A Compilation Of Inspired Sermons

William D. Hutchinson

Table of Contents

Section 2

To Established And Potential Leaders

Section 3

Social Issues For All Sectors Of Society

Preface

On numerous occasions when I preached, persons requested my sermon outlines, on other occasions they taped them and have sought my permission to send them to their family members and friends. That is one of the things that influenced my decision to compile them and to make them available to a wider audience, than those in my immediate reach. I hope that my offerings will impact lives in positive ways that will inspire other ministers and ministerial aspirants to a greater commitment in whatever they do.

Some are privileged to travel extensively with the gospel, some have only been able to assist others to go, but they themselves have never gone anywhere, however, in order to fulfill the great commission, which was written to the disciples and is recorded in **St. Matthew 28: 16-20 (NIV)** "Make disciples for the kingdom" I honestly believe that I am obligated to reach others even beyond my present region. It is with this in mind that I wrote these sermons, and hope that those who read them will be touched and be stirred to action.

Way back in my childhood days, at a point when I had no clue whatsoever that I would become a Minister of the Gospel, others saw something in me that I was not able to see, so, their assessment of me has now come to full view, that the vision that they had was for this appointed time.

A full explanation of my Life and works, along with my profile is outlined in my previous Book, entitled: **"Autobiography and Pictorial of a Fulfilled Life, By: Rev. William. D. Hutchinson"** I hope you will want to read it also, to get a background to my Life story and my Ministry, for further access to my other books I can be contacted at: 876-383-1454. I look forward to you helping me to reach others.

GOD BLESS.

Congratulations

Congratulations and Commendations are in order for Reverend William D Hutchinson an ordained Bishop and Parish Overseer in the Church of God of Prophecy on the publishing of his third book. I would like to describe him as an accomplished author, having written other books on Marriage and Family Life. On this occasion he has used the opportunity to share his inspired, dynamic and motivational sermons with the world by moving from the spoken word to the printed word. Hence a "Compilation of Inspired Sermons" is his latest work and it has sermons which speak to the Laity, Leaders and social issues in the wider society. The sermons are timely and relevant as Christian themes and doctrines are addressed, along with current and topical issues in the society. Thank you man of God for sharing your heart with us as the Lord has spoken to you over the years. I am happy to say that absence from your Sunday Morning service will not deny us access to your sermons.

Bishop Dr. Franklyn Beckford D. Min J.P.

Dedication and Thanks

Thanks to the following persons:

- My Late mother: Sister Janet (Mama) of Marlie Hill Manchester (for my upbringing)
- My dear wife and life partner: Arlene (For helping me to stay on the right track)
- My daughter: Karlene & husband Mario, my sister-in-law: Melva, and my niece: Nekeisha, for assisting me in the dotting of the: I's and the crossing of the Ts.
- To my daughter: Kadeen and her three children: Jonathan, Raheem and Kaleica.
- Bishop Ronald J. McFarlane (former Parish Overseer of Clarendon South and pastor of the 30A Fernleigh Avenue church, May Pen, Clarendon. COGOP. (Who identified the ministerial call in me.
- My cousin: Minister Leon M. Langley: former minister at the Marlie Hill Church, Manchester COGOP, now pastor of the Nomprel church, Manchester COGOP. Who first acknowledged the ministerial call in me.
- My sisters: Hermina & Naina, my brothers: Huglen and Eric
- My two pastorates: Hayes & Bustamante Highway COGOP.
- And my area of administration: Clarendon South; for the support they gave me throughout my ministerial experiences.

Section 1
To All Persons, Especially To The Laity

Chapter 1
Encouragement To Righteous Living

Read: Joshua 01:07-09 In the book of Joshua, God's encouragement to him regarding steadfastness, straightforwardness and prosperity. It is interesting to note that those well sort for blessings are hinged on our obedience to God (obeying the book of law) it is however interesting to note that some of us sometimes want the prosperity, but are not willing to do what the process demands in order to reap the full benefits.

Joshua upon succeeding Moses in 1451 BC., he observed the mentality of the Israelites, and had to address the situation in order to change the outcome, some of us are not willing to do what the process demands rather we can be very vocal about not receiving the expected result, there is carnal mindedness and there is spiritual mindedness, each has its own reward. We may not reveal our secrets, rather we utter other than trueness in order to achieve our desired goal. If through deception we obtain positions or status, those things will give results, but only for a short time, because, God is no respecter of persons. Knowing that, "With what-ever ye mete it shall be measured to us again". **St. Mark 04: 24.** Jacob tricked Isaacs his father, to get his brother Esau's birthright, as a playback to him, after serving Laban for seven years in .order to have his daughter Rachel for his wife, he was given Leah instead. (According to the custom of the land) Genesis 29:01-30. Later he tricked his father-in-law Laban; (who is also his uncle) Genesis 29:10-21, and Genesis 30: 25-43 states that Jacob tricked Laban and took his strongest cattle, the state of sowing and reaping was played out to Jacob, he tricked his father Isaac, then he was tricked by Laban his Father-in-law. So, he tricked his father-in- law at a time when Laban did not expect it; and the list continued.

Righteous living is not convenience; it is doing the right things at all times, regardless of the outcome. (The word righteous means: equitable living, to be morally right, even if it is legally wrong. for something can be legally right yet it is morally wrong, or just not expedient, eg. paying the utmost farthing; no mercy, or not being **straight,** these days everybody has rights so, they want to be allowed to do what-ever they please.)

Living: **W**hen the word is used as a noun, it speaks of the basic necessities of life, or the standard of **living**, good living is life at a higher order, or luxurious living, that which Kirk Nugent speaks of: how "he wants to die living."

Living: when used as an adjective: refers to those now alive, or of water perennially flowing (lasting through all seasons of the year, lasting long or forever)

Isaiah 53:01-12 (712 B.C. The prophet complains of the want of faith and the suffering of Christ)

St. Luke 02:1-14 (Speaks of the birth of Christ, The journey to Bethlehem of Mary and Joseph to pay their taxes, regardless of Mary's advance state of pregnancy. Mary; Joseph's wife, Jesus' mother, this speaks to the point that our situations gives no excuse, to vital duties and functions, some of us love to make excuses, when some simple things occur.

Can we just pause to imagine, the odd and extreme processes that the birth, the life journey, the sufferings of Jesus, His death, burial and resurrection among many other things caused, before His eventual triumph and His ascension, note that success is never an accident, but rather the result of intelligent efforts. Let all of us, each of us, do introspection today, regarding our patience during our life journey. We don't want to be processed, rather just reward us, because reward is what we want, for example, poor Mary the mother of Jesus, what an embarrassment, a virgin to be giving birth, that was not something that Mary planned, not to mention Joseph. There were whispers all around town, up town, down town, in town and round town. Joseph professed to be all that and more, yet the virgin girl he boasted about is now pregnant, so if it is not him then who?! Can you just imagine the scandal in town?

Reading: Joshua 01: 7-9:

These verses speaks of God's encouragement to steadfastness, straightforwardness and prosperity, those well sort for blessings are hinged on our obedience to God (obeying the book of the law). It is interesting to note that some of us sometimes want the prosperity but are not willing to do what the process demand?

Joshua upon succeeding Moses in **1451 B.C.,** observed the mentality of the Israelites, he had to address the situation in order to change the outcome, some of us, sometimes are not willing to do what the process demands, rather we can be very vocal about not receiving the expected results, without honestly, thinking that the action is what drives the results. There is carnal mindedness and there is Spiritual mindedness, each has its own, we may not reveal our secrets, but may utter other than trueness in order to achieve a desired goal, if through deception we obtain positions, status, things those will give results, but only for a short time, because God is no respecter of persons, Eg. Jacob tricked Isaacs his father to get his Brother Esau's birth-right, and later Laban his son-in-law tricked him with his cattle. The state of congruence played out on him, something he did not expect, more-so from his father-in-law and especially at that time.

Righteous living is not convenience; it is doing the right things at all times regardless of the outcome. (The word righteous: is equitable living, to be morally right, even if it is legally wrong. For something can be legally right yet morally wrong, or just not expedient. Example, Paying the utmost farthing; no mercy, or not being **STRAIGHT,** these days everybody has rights.)

Living: when viewed **as** a noun speaks of the basic necessities of life, or the standard of living, Good living, is life at a higher order; luxurious living, that which Kirk Nugent speaks of: "he want to die living"

Living: when used as an adjective: refers to those now alive, or of water perennially flowing (lasting through all seasons of the year, lasting long or forever)

Read Proverbs 03:5-6. From the wise-man's perspective speaks of: one's trust in God, self confidence, guidance and a testimony, and further states that the result will always be different, when things are done wholeheartedly.

I cannot overemphasize the wholehearted approach to doing things especially for the Lord.

Wholeheartedness: Giving God wholehearted worship.

- In Love (According to Deuteronomy 06:09)
- In Obedience (According to Psalm 119:02)
- In Trust (With reference to Proverbs 03:05)
- In Prayer (As stated by Jeremiah 29:13)
- In Repentance (Clearly put Joel 02:12)

Serving Others Wholeheartedly Amid the Pressure of Duty

- It burns like in inward fire (Jeremiah 20:09)

- It calls like the voice of a lion (Acts 03:08)
- It Binds the Soul to its Task (St. Luke 12:50)
- It Urges Us to Haste (St. John 09:04)
- It makes the Message imperative (Acts 04: 20)
- And Sounds like Woes in the ears of him who falters (1st. Corinthians 9:16)

Righteous living is a lifestyle, a fully dedicated life to the cause of God, subjecting and subduing desires to His will, and anticipates a favorable outcome.

Will you make such a dedication to Him today?

Who will say, I am committed?

Chapter 2
Making The Path Of Righteousness Your Christian Walk

Reading: Psalm 23:01-06

This is a Psalm of David it was written between 1440 B.C and 586 B.C. (8554years) by about 7 different groups)

The book of Psalms although poetic in nature and Style also includes some contents that are used by believers when crying out to God from the depth of despair, to singing to God in the heights of celebration, and chant against the enemy when danger assail, whether in danger, despairing or rejoicing they can be used to make honest expressions to God. When we need comfort for sure then Psalm 23 is certainly the place to go.

David who was a shepherd by profession, used the most familiar term in order to get his message across in the easiest way, he relate to them (his country –men) by using the sheep and shepherd's perspective, although he spoke from in the temple mostly.

Psalm 23 is one of the most popularly used Psalm I would like to dissect this **theme** a little for simplicity

Eg: Path is to walk like Righteousness is to Christians

Psalm 01 (I quote: "Blessed is the man that walketh not in the counsels of the ungodly nor standeth in the ways of Sinners, nor sitteth in the seat of the scornful."

The word **path** appears 72 times in the English bible: 68 times in the OT and 04 times in the New, each time it appears in the NT it refers to "making your path straight"

In the OT Psalm 16:11 and I quote "Thou wilt shew me the **path** of life, in thy presence is fullness of joy and at His right hand there are pleasures for evermore."

The word Righteousness appears 291 times in the English bible, 200 times in the OT and 91 times in the New. And always points to: blessings and rejoicing and at the same time, carries with it some consequences.

In these instances **our walk** is synonymous to miracles and signs and are assigned mostly to us Christians.

Eg: Being a Visionary; seeing men walking as men and not as trees. **Mark 08:24**

The blind man sees, and glorified God. **Matthew 15:31**

The dumb speak the lame walk. **Matthew 15:31**

Peter Walking on the sea. **Mark 06:48-49**

Or not **walking** according to the tradition of men. **Mark 07:05**

Or walk in the commandments and ordinances of our Lord blamelessly: **Luke 01:06**

Psalm 23:04 Yea though I walk through the valley of the shadow of death, I will fear no evil. That was an area between Jerusalem and Jericho and a deep rift between the Jews and the Samaritans; according to **Luke 10:27-37**

"Death cast a frightening shadow over us, because we are entirely helpless in its presence, then we can struggle with other enemies, such as: pain, suffering, fear, and diseases" then and there only one person can walk us through death's dark valley and brings us safely on the other side; That is the God of life: The Good Shepherd who offers us eternal life.

That sounds very nice and comforting but we must conform to him before we get to that valley so that our relationship with him will be well established. We need to have a friend before we really need one.

Abraham **Genesis 17:01** "And when Abraham was ninety years old and nine the Lord appeared to Abraham and said unto him, I am the Almighty God, walk before me and be though perfect."

There are persons who have distinguished themselves by their Christian walk.   **As Patriarchs**

Enoch: In his walk with God, please Him and witnessed for Him according to**: Genesis 05:24**

Noah: He built the ark for the safety of the Chosen, **Genesis 05:22-24** He also built an alter and offered sacrifice. **Genesis 08:20**

Abraham: Being the father of a multitude, The Spiritual Pilgrims and answered the divine call. **Genesis 12:01**

Isaac: The long looked for son who was peaceable, prayerful and a man of great faith Genesis 26:20-22, 25, Hebrews 11:20

Jacob: The Supplanter (son of Isaac) **Genesis 32:09-12**

Some Prominent Women

Abigail: One of David's wife 1st Samuels 25:03

Deborah: One of Israel's judges (A Patriotic woman who was associated with Barak in Judging Israel.)

Esther: A woman of beauty Ester 02:07, Of self denial and heroism. Esther 04: 16

Hannah: Hannah was one of Elkanah's wives, and the mother of the Prophet Samuel, who was the product of his mother's powerful silent prayer, she was praised for her prayerfulness and self denial. She was very thankful. 1st. Samuels 01: 10,11

Hulder: Was a prophetess 2nd Kings 22:14

Mirriam: She was the sister of Moses, she was ambitious, vigorous and musical, a leader of Israel Exodus 15:21

The Queen of Sheba: She made a notable visited King Solomon 1st Kings10:01

Ruth: The woman of constancy, filial love, industriousness and piety. Ruth 02:06-07

Sarah: The wife of Abraham and the mother of nations, beautiful, inpatient of divine favours, and had a ruling personality in the home. Genesis 21: 10-12

Dorcas: She was the benevolent woman of Joppa. Acts 09:36

Elizabeth: Was the mother of John the Baptist who was the fore-runner of Jesus. St. Luke 01:05

Martha: Martha then worried house Keeper from Bethany who was the sister of Mary and lazarus, she was hospitable and, anxious and full of faith. St. Luke 10:50

Mary: The mother of Jesus, a woman of faith and piety, spiritual minded and maternal love. St. John 19:25

Priscilla: The wife of Aquila: they were they were laborers with Paul they were both banished from Rome. Acts 18:02,26

Salome: Salome was the mother of James and John St. Mark 15:40

The Genesis 3:8 Account says: God have a way of walking in the garden in the cool of the day, he walk, he check when you are so relaxed and not expecting Him. What If He walk in your garden today what will He find you in good shape?

Galatians 05:16 "Walk in the spirit and you shall not fulfill the lust of the flesh."

Chapter 3
Using Today's Standards To Judge Behaviors Of Yesteryears

Scripture Readings:

Titus 02: 6-7 "Young men likewise exhort to be sober minded. In all things showing thyself a pattern of good works, in doctrine showing incorruptness, gravity and sincerity"

The NIV further amplified the point that in the ancient Greek society husband / fathers did not carry out their functional responsibilities as they should, therefore we through learning, must exceed their standards, we must train our children well, because we have seen in the recent past, where persons were invited to positions of prominence, and were denied by societal outcry, for things that were done during youthful days, (decades ago) and the accused thought, that those things were forgotten, and in their own defense even stated in the two most recent accounts, both accused could not recall doing those things, and others merely escaped similar fate, Youthful exuberance caused persons to do things they later regret, upon the reflection of the mature minds, because of things which they did without weighing the consequences before doing the act.; we must be cultured to take responsibility for actions, because ignorance is no excuse. And most time the accused thought they would not be caught or being brought to books, in that setting they would have escaped the consequences equivalent to the act.

The secular world is so different from the spiritual world, in that, once an acknowledgment is made for wrong doings, confession, forsaking and the turning away from the practice, and forgiveness is sought, then, God forgives, dropped the charges and wiped the guilt away, and replaces the accusation with innocence, and remove the person or persons into a brand new realm, While in the secular world, once there are substantial evidences being brought to bear, then consequences of today will be meted out to the accused even though the act was done long time ago.

The worse part of that process is that, today's consequences may be, and can be in excess and far more stringent than they were at the time when the act or acts were committed. I hereby suggest to my listeners and or my readers, let us be careful of what we do, say, or get involved in, because we may later live to regret them, be guided by this thought: "If it is not right, don't do it; if it is not true don't say it" and this is regardless of age or status.

I have been privilege to speak with someone who confessed to have made very costly mistakes, done under the guise of youthful mistake by being involved sexually with someone with whom there were no previous relationship, that it wasn't the type of person he would want to or have any long-term relationship with, more so to be the mother of his child, but ended up with a physically challenged child that he will have to maintain for the rest of his life; this is a serious and very costly lesson that comes with a very high price, (A few minutes of pleasure delivered a lifetime expenses) and demand quality time to spend with him, and attend to a child *under* the heading of fairness to both the mother and the child, (especially with that condition with which the child was born, demands a greater than the average attention and finances) we ought to be living today for tomorrow, so that when tomorrow comes, we will have no need to want to run away from it. When God orders one's step the outcome is always different. The blessings of the Lord maketh rich and adds no sorrow. ....

Youthful exuberance will not be an excuse for substandard behavior, this has been proven that even though Solomon had more than equal opportunities, he was the wisest of all men and had more that average opportunity, there is a consequence for every action, yet with choice comes responsibility. So. If you are young take heed, if you are more mature, then please help me in sending this message, that with choice, comes responsibility, none shall escape.

Logically if we set out on any given path, it will only take us to its destination

And unless we change course that's where we will end up. It is said: "first we make our habits, then our habits make us, after we are made, and are in a place of influence, then usually we pass on the traits to others, because behavior is learnt, when we have touched the lives of others in positive ways then we can be assured that we are sowing into a good harvest.

Conclusion

Think of Solomon, how much more privileged than others he was.

- He enjoyed a home surrounded by both fortunes and misfortunes and where polygamy was preached and jealousy and strife were practiced.
- He ascended to the throne of his father David at a tender age and, there he made some terrible mistakes example (1) he married the daughter of a heathen king. (Pharaoh) (2) he had a moral downfall with many women.
- He was vested with wisdom (he was the wisest of all men a title he still maintain)
- He was honored for the honorable visit he got from the Queen of Sheba.

- Yet although he was so wise, so honored, so privilege, so powerful and so famous, he had a moral downfall with women and Idolatry and ended up in uncertainity.

Chapter 4
Stages Of Spiritual Growth, Where Are You?

Read St. Matthew 13:01-08

Stage: Phase, arena, point, or period

Growth: Expansion, development, enlargement, intensification

Introduction

The passage of scripture being discoursed today, speaks to spiritual receptivity and not just to selective seed droppings. (The point is, choices come with responsibility: He that has an ear to hear, let him hear.) Please note that the words SEED SOWING is mentioned in the Bible **257** times, but it is only **21** of the **257** times that it refers to crops or plants the other **236** times it refers to one's offspring (People) I will give the references as follows: **06** times in the **O.T.** and **15** times in the **N.T.**

In the **O.T. (Regarding Crops)**

Genesis 01:11

Genesis 01:12

Genesis 01:29

Genesis 08:22

Isaiah   55:10

Jeremiah 50:16

In the N.T.

> **St. Matthew 13: 03**
>
> **St. Matthew 13:18**
>
> **St. Mark 04: 03**
>
> **St. Mark 04:14**
>
> **St. Luke 08:05**
>
> **2nd. Corinthians 09:10**

It has become clearer in my mind that each time I researched the scriptures. I found it to be inexhaustible. So the more one research, and the more knowledge one gains, is the better able one should be, to adhering to the word, by applying it to one's life and enabling one to divide it rightly. That in turn should enhance spiritual health, spiritual growth and victories in light of seed sowing as it relates to crops and plants, when used to relate to others regarding services, duties and lifestyle, or reaping what one sows, along with the urgency with which we do things all these and more should assist in the commanding of the attention of the listeners and readers of this material, that will assist in the changing effects that the words imposed on one's life. **St. Matthew 13:23.**

Dr. Luke said in Luke **10:38**. When Jesus visited the home of his late friend Lazarus in Bethany He made a comparison between Mary and Martha. Martha complained to Jesus about Mary, while she sat at his feet capitalizing on the moment to draw from Him the things that matter most. After which Jesus told Martha that Mary has chosen the good part that shall not be taken away from her. Then later she went and sat with them.

In Acts 02:41 The apostle Paul expounded on the subject **as** follows: Seed sowing and the level of productivity, are based on how gladly one receives the word; and He further states that on the same day that they received the word they were baptized and the same day they were added to the Church about 3,000 souls. The word gladly is defined as follows: willingly, happily with pleasure, with joy and cheerfulness. How are you receiving the word today are you taking it with gladness?. What stage are you today, and are you conscious and honest enough, as to whether or not, you are growing at comparable rate and speed?

Productivity is more than just scattering the seeds, feasibility studies should first be done by persons with the right skill-set as to whether or not the soil is ideal for the type of seeds one intends to Sow. Then that information is ascertained then soil preparation is done and plans be put in place for the maintenance of the plant, if one expects to have a good yield. My personal experience recently is about a crop of callaloo I planted in a box at home. It was so lovely, that when I reaped it the first time, I expected to reap more times based on the nature of the plant, but that was not forthcoming. So I went to the agricultural shop and sought information as to how to enhance the yield. A product was introduced to me at which point I sprayed and mulched the plant. Having done that my expectation was raised, but much to my disappointment, instead of an enhancement of productivity, they faded and eventually died   (I later learnt that I over mulched it)

Spiritual growth is compared to the sowing and reaping of the natural plants, as to how best to maximize the level of productivity, much is dependent on whether the seeds are sewn on good ground, stony ground, shallow grown, fall by the wayside or fall among thorns. Also how it is maintained and protected from insect and pests that can retard the growth or destroy the plants completely.

Regardless of how skilfully we evangelized our area, we need to realize that according to the song: "We plough the field and scatter the good seed on the land, but it is fed and watered by God's Almighty hand." We may learn new and innovative ways to do things, or may be able to place special emphasis on our work, and might even be able to divide the Scriptures rightly; but unless God is the center of our work, and our worship to Him is done in sincerity, and in the way that is totally acceptable to Him then more-so that we resist the temptation to become the center of attraction may be by our dressing, our bodily activities, or any other thing that will shift the attention of those we seek to lead from God to us. Because everything we do in worship must be designed to give glory to God, and not to impress men. As it relates to our growth we must measure ourselves and our work with the Scriptures and stay in line with it. If we humble ourselves before Him then he will raise us up to new levels in His kingdom.

Conclusion

The **Galatians 04:08-09** state finally brethren,

Whatsoever things are true, whatsoever things are honest?

Whatsoever things are just, whatsoever things are pure?

Whatsoever things are lovely, whatsoever things are of good report?

It there be any virtue, and if there be any praise, think on these things

V.9 those things which he has both learned and received and heard, and seen in me, do: and the God of Peace shall be with you.

Chapter 5
Taming The Untamable

Read Ephesians 04:11-16 (Members of the Body of Christ)

From the Vietnamese Potbellied Pigs to Siberian Foxes which were both very wile animals, but both have now become emotionally friendly, because humans have learnt how to tame them, and have enjoyed, and are enjoying doing so. Example monkeys were trained to act in Commercials, and deer to eat out of human hands, such interactions were once unheard of.

So **James** puts it this way, all kinds of animals: birds, reptiles and sea creatures are being tamed by mankind, but there is something we are unable to tame, all of us put together are still having big trouble getting the tongue under control. According to James Chapter 03:01-12, sp. Vs.5-7 (speaking specifically of the human tongue.) From AD 49 (1,970 years ago) and to this date the human tongue is still running wild.

James being the brother of Jesus, and one of the Christian leaders in the Jerusalem Church, a first Century Christian Leader, who resided in the Gentile communities outside of Palestine, wrote because he was disturbed of the brethrens behavior and wrote of the importance of Controlling the tongue (Speech Control).

My Thought

"If it is not right don't do it

If it is not true, don't say it

And if it is not safe, avoid it."

Although our words may be on the tip of our tongue, they originate from the heart, the tongue only speaks what the heart is full of; The same tongue can do both good and evil **V9.** One scholar Peter David once said, on one hand the tongue is very religious, and on the other hand it is most profane, so if we cannot tame the unruly tongue of ours, it is destined to give trouble daily.

According to **Psalm 141:03** Only God can tame the untamable, He can set a guard over our mouth, and keep a watch over the door of our lips.

It took the experts thousands of years to domesticate the dogs. And the dogs are man's best friend.

Thought: To rule the tongue, let God rule your heart.

Chapter 6
Being Sensitive To The Enemies Devices

Much is said in the bible about the enemies, because from the beginning of time God's chosen people had enemies; Enemies are usually persons who are hostile, who are against you, usually they armed with weapons, or information about you that can be used to either disrupt or destroy your life, they may even find other individuals, groups or institutions that oppose your views to join forces against you.

Much is said in 2$^{nd.}$ **Samuels 05: 17–25** concerning David and the Army of the Philistines, there were long running battles between the Israelites and the Philistines. When the Philistines heard that David was appointed king over Israel their anger raged, and they went in search for him. David went down to his stronghold and sought the Lord's direction on the way forward, the Lord gave him a timely command for him to take on the enemies and David acted accordingly and he was victorious over his enemies.

The accounts given in the English Bible concerning **enemies**, is extremely high, it is stated **244** times in the Old Testament and **19** times in the New Testament, totaling **263** times all together.

One can just imagine a shepherd boy became king over Judah, then king over all Israel, obviously a spate of jealousy came into play from the other kings of the area, because the other kings were more or less born as princes or got the position by marring into a Royal Family, but this David was called from the back side of the desert to the palace. (The difference is that was a divine call)

David's father: Jessie, he did not see the kingly potential in his youngest son either, in-fact, he ignored the possibility of him being selected as Judah's king. **1ˢᵗ· Chronicles 02:13-14** mentioned his seven sons, while "**1ˢᵗ· Samuel 17:12-13** mentioned eight" one thing was for sure, the other brothers did not fit the kingly profile, from the **first** one being: Eliab, **the 2ⁿᵈ·** Abinadab, **3ʳᵈ·** Shimea, **4ᵗʰ·** Nethanel, **5ᵗʰ·** Raddai, **6ᵗʰ·** Ozem; but David the **7ᵗʰ·;** he was the chosen one. Note (They also had 2 sisters: Zeruiah and Abigail)

David's victories did not come easily he had struggles, in one instant he left the flock he was assigned to attend to, and went down where the battle was arrayed between Israel and the Philistines to investigate the status of the battle, his eldest brother Eliab saw him and said what are you doing here, who is attending to the flock in your absence? Do you not care about them anymore? His brother did not think he should have left the flock for any reason at all. 1ˢᵗ· Samuels 01-10 tells us of the successes that David had during the time when his heart was right with his God, while Chapters 11-24 tells of his struggles after he committed sin with Bathsheba then tried to cover it up. He put Bathaheba's husband Uriah, at the fore front of the battle where he was killed; Although his sins were forgiven the consequences remained; for which he encountered trouble and distress, both with his family and the nations. Nb. covering one's sins will only multiply the consequences painfully.

David was victorious during the times when his heart was in tune with God but as soon as he resorted to his lustful desires, he started losing the battles. In order for us to have victories over the enemy we should not only capitalize on the known weakness of the enemy, or be carried away by our known strength, rather we must rely on the leading of the Lord. According to **1ˢᵗ· Samuels 17:24** being a cowardice or being powerless does not stand anyone engaged in battle, in good stead, rather as the thought goes: "if we think we are powerless, then we are twice defeated in the battles of life."

When David was about to face Goliath he knew the strength and accomplishments of the giant, but he also knew the Strength of the Almighty God. His power along and His greatness, therefore David took his staff, his sling and his five stones along with his script, and drew near unto the Philistine. He knew very well that his natural ability was not enough; because he served the All-Powerful one, he faced the giant with the confidence that he would be victorious. See: **1st. Samuels 17:38–58.**

Psalm 23: 01- 06 speaks of the greatness and mercies of God, toward David, while being a shepherd, and later on when he became king.

Approximately 1440 B.C. David fought with Saul, and in **Psalm 23** he made a deep expression of God's goodness to him, not only for protection, but also for the very rich opportunities that were afforded him. The message puts it this way: With God as my shepherd I don't need a thing. You have bedded me down in lush meadows. You find me quiet pools to drink from and true to your word, You let me catch my breath and send me in the right direction; even when the way goes through death's valley, I am not afraid when You walk by my side. Your trusty shepherd's crook, makes me feel secure.

You serve me a six course dinner, right in front of my enemies,

You revive my drooping head,

My cup brims with blessings.

Your beauty and love chase after me, every day of my life.

I am home again in the house of God, for the rest of my life.

A six course dinner is not a popular type of meal; it is usually prepared by the affluent, for the affluent. God will not only give us the victories over the enemies in the physical battles, but like David he will give us victories over: sickness, poverty, fear, insecurity, poor self esteem, weakness of the flesh and He will elevate us to levels beyond our imagination.

David's God is our God. Trust Him!

Chapter 7
Rejoicing In The Confidence Of Your Faith

Rejoicing is one thing almost everyone wants to have, at some point or other; to rejoice about anything on occasions when there are aspects of uncertainty regarding the reason for rejoicing; it can limit the extent of one' rejoicing. When one rejoices with confidence then it makes a great deal of difference. David had an occasion of confidence in God at a time when he was at great risk with his enemies. In **Psalm 118:07-09** and he wrote: "Therefore shall I see my desire upon them that hate me. It is better to trust in the Lord than to put confidence in man, or put confidence in princes, then later in the same discourse he said: **Verse 23 -24** he said, "the Lord's doing is marvelous in our eyes, but on this day that the Lord has made, I will rejoice and be glad in it; because the stone which was rejected by the builders has now become the head of the corner.

People put their trust in different people, things and institutions, **Psalm 118:08-09 NIV** "Pilots put confidence in their planes, commuters place their confidence in trains, buses and car, sometimes we don't see the drivers of those equipment, most times we don't know them, yet we trust them to take us to our destinations, if we can trust someone, or something that much, how much more willing should be to trust God, to guide us through this life to an eternal destination.

A prince is a male heir to the throne of his or her majesty, whose duty is to support him or her as the focal point of a national pride, his duty includes the following: Bringing people together across all sector of society, representing stability and continuity in the kingdom, and highlighting achievements and emphasizing it with great importance, and do so with national pride, with the primary purpose being to make his boss look good.

The buoyancy, assurance and belief that a prince has in the head of the monarchy gives great confidence to him on almost all matters of importance; this can only be liken unto the trust Christians should have in God. Faith is more than just trust, it is strong confidence and belief in a superior power; In the Christian religion, the Jewish faith, Islam or any religion, faith is the underlining factor. **2nd. Corinthians 05:07** states: "For we walk by faith and not by sight."   And **St. Matthew 21:21** speaks to faith as much as a mustard seed, and say we can move mountains.

The Dictionary of Doctrinal Words, states with reference to: John Scott who said "Faith is a reasoning trust, which rest thoughtfully and confidently upon the trustworthiness of God, which is not a blind faith, It is the substance of things hoped for, the evidence of things not seen the according to **Hebrews 11:01** (which means proof, or proving, in the Christian sense, faith may be defined as a conscious mental desire to do the will of God. Further to that the Christian faith has two main components **(1)** Trust or acceptance, belief that Jesus is Lord with acknowledgment of His resurrection and **(2)** intellectual content, the revealed truth that is firmly believed and is reflected in the life of the believer.

I order to acquire this type of faith the **St. Matthew 17:20-21** account must be applied "This kind cometh not but by prayer and fasting" in order for the theme to come alive fully in our lives then "Rejoicing" which is: elation, joy, delight, exultation, jubilee and satisfaction or great expression of satisfaction, either for achievement and fortune gained or for the downfall or failures of individuals and or systems that worked against us.

I will venture to express my humble opinion on joy and happiness; Joy which is a part of rejoicing has only three layers on the vertical plain, while happiness has nine, yet when compared; joy is smaller yet stronger, because happiness only last as long as the happening; but joy comes from God, so if I am to choose between happiness and joy. I will go for joy, for the joy of the Lord is my strength.

	H
	A
	P
	P
	I
	N
J	E
O	S
Y	S

God Bless!

Chapter 8
Habits And Addictions

Scripture Readings Philippians 04:04 - 09

1st Corinthians 16:15 "I beseech you, brethren, (ye know the house of Steph'anas, that it is the first fruit A-cha'ia, and that they have *addicted* themselves to the Ministry of the saints.)

Habits: Behavior, lifestyle, way of life, routine, practice.

The Dictionary of Doctrinal Words puts it this way, (It is a Latin word) "Habit" meaning to have, it is a condition of character, or the way one conducts him or herself, it is the prevailing disposition of a person's feelings or thoughts, it can be a behavior pattern which by frequently repetition has become nearly or completely involuntary, habits often have negative meanings, connotations or flaws in character, but habits can also be good but for Christians they should result in proper discipline and Christian living. It is also said, that if you do something twenty-one times it becomes a habit *(habits are easy to make, but hard to break)* therefore we should practice holiness until it becomes a habit or a lifestyle.

Thought: "First you make your habits, then your habits make you."

Addiction: Is an obsession, infatuation, dependency, crave, need.

According to Wendy Wood Research Psychologist and Author of: "Good Habits, Bad habits on Quora" bad habits, by definition are thing we wish we didn't do, but not all bad habits are equal, example: "nail biding, though annoying and embarrassing it may be, smoking is a habit that is significantly worse for our health, Substance use disorders resemble bad habits gone amok. Addiction threatens the health of the individuals involved as well as those around them. Ultimately its ills effects will harm the entire society.

These two: (habit and addiction) can become both positive features of our lives like the house of Step'hanas who addicted themselves to the ministry of the saints. So we should make every last effort to practice the good things, Paul said to the Corinthians as is recorded in 1st . Corinthians 15:58: "Therefore My beloved brethren be ye steadfast, unmovable, always abounding in the work of the Lord, for as much as ye know that your labour is not in vain in the Lord."

The word LABOUR is an English word, but the Americans took "U" out of it, and so it is now LABOR without "U' and that is why some of us don't want to do anything! Not even in the Church or the kingdom.

Christians should have:

- **Willing hands**, so that the work of the Church is not a burden to just a few.
- **Swift feet**; willing enough to bring the message of the King to the lost and dying.
- Trained ears that doesn't like gossip but listening to the Voice of God and the call of his people (sometimes for help)
- The eyes of the visionaries: to see the harvest field so white and ready to be harvest and clear vision for the direction of the Lord.
- **Melodious voices**: Ready and willing to sing harmoniously the praises to the King.
- The wisdom and the skillfulness of leadership that is required in such a perilous time like this.

- Clean hearts to be the Royal Throne from which the good Lord will live and reign.

Then when all these and more are done, we will be sure to reap our eternal rewards.

Perfection is the hallmark' of the Church and it is attainable (when holiness becomes a habit in our lives then that is human-perfection. It is so hard to cure a person from addictions; usually the doctors have to use the same type of substances that the patient is addicted to. By using reduced proportion and then phased out its use gradually,

Finally by brethren, let us seek to be addicted to true worship, right Christian living, the right life style, love the brotherhood, have peace with God and with our fellowmen and enjoy the fellowship of which we are a part. At is usually at this point of our live that maturity is achieved. Let us thrive for it.

Chapter 9
There Is No Mercy Outside Of God's Judgment

Read: Nehemiah 07:3 "The gates of Jerusalem are not to be opened until the sun is hot, while the gatekeepers are still on duty, have them shut the doors and bar them also appoint residents of Jerusalem as guards, some at their post and some near their own houses"

The rules that govern the city of Jerusalem had no authority in the adjacent cities, it was intended for that city alone, it is clear that kingdom citizens should uphold the rules of the kingdom and remain protected. Let us not take the risk, because it will not be worth it, for what shall it profit us to gain the whole world and loose his soul (and in some cases his or her life) the discourse in **St. Matthew 19:24** concerning the rich young ruler and the eye of the needle, speaks to the fact that the reason the reference was made, is that once the gates of Jerusalem were shut, before the merchants get in, who-ever decide not to take the risks of staying outside the city walls of Jerusalem in order to protect their merchandize, would be at great risk, otherwise would have to leave the camel and the merchandize and squeeze through the eye of the needle into the city (the safe area). *(That small gate to the City; according to 9th & 15th. century history allude to the fact that it existed, although there is no widely accepted evidence of the existence of such gate in Jerusalem)* (Matthew Henry's Commentary on **St. Mark 10:24-27** refers to a small straight gate to Jerusalem and translate the stated camel, to a cable rope that must be untwisted to single Strawn, in order to go through the eye of the needle) It is usually hard to give up great riches and it is also difficult to serve two masters at the same time, Nb. Money can be a good

41

servant but a bad master. It is always a difficult decision to make but a valuable one, whether to sell out and be safe, or retain it and be at risk, Be careful to note however that there are great dangers outside of God's judgment and the only safe realm available to mankind, is to live in the will of God.

Mercy: Is defined by the English Dictionary as follows: Compassion, Pity, clemency, sympathy, understanding, or leniency shown to another who is in his power, and has no claim to kindness, it is God's forbearance and forgiveness for sin.

Judgment: Is, the sentence of the court of justice, decisions by a judge, ruling, finding, verdict, result, opinion, and conclusion.

These two key words are opposite in meaning and stands firmly regarding consequences. God's mercies are from everlasting to everlasting and endures forever. **(Psalm 136: 01)   James 02:13 States:** "He shall have judgment without mercy, that hath shown no mercy, and mercy rejoiced against judgment." According to **1st. Peter 4:17** Judgment will first begins in the house of God, the **NIV** says: this is not the final judgment "the family of God" we all can sin while still being Christians, but we always will face the consequence, this comes to show, that if consequences are metered out to the believers, then how much more will the unbeliever's consequences be.

Some Christians take the chance to sin and pray, and sin again, experimenting with the mercies of God, the scripture says in **St. Luke 12:47-48** The servant which knew his Lord's will and prepared not himself, shall be beaten with many stripes, but he that knew not, and commit things worthy of stripes, shall be beaten with few stripes. (**The Message** say "He or She shall be thoroughly trashed, or receive a slap on the hand) We have to be careful not to become presumptuous before a Just God; because God is no respecter of persons, His judgments are as sure as His mercies, no wonder we see some things happen to some people and we wonder, and wonder again, because persons who continue to experiment with God's mercy usually reap the extent of his wrath, let us learn from their mistakes and line up right with God. (Stay in the safe zone.)

The word mercy appears **262** times in the English Bible (**208** times in the Old Testament and **54** times in the new. While the word Judgment appears **408** times in the English Bible: (**329** in the Old Testament and **79** times in the New Testament) clearly mercy and judgment are mentioned so many times, the repetitiveness suggests both abundance and availability, but God said clearly in **Nahum 01:06** "who can stand before His indignation and who can abide the fierceness of His anger? His fury is poured out like fire, and the rocks are thrown down by Him. **Romans 06:23** says: "For the wages of sin is death, but the gift of God is eternal life through Jesus Christ our Lord." Christians who have enjoyed both the face and the hand of the Lord should know the extent of his power and should only want the His blessings and mercies, not His judgments nor His anger.

Mercy is available while we abide in the realm of His precepts, and His judgment is activated once we go outside of it, on the inside of the Realms of His judgment there is mercy, is security, prosperity, the joy of the Lord, and hope which make us not ashamed, and there is no risk because in the presence of the Lord is fullness of Joy and at his right hand there are pleasures forevermore. Outside of God's will, the risk is so high, the temptation is so great, the failure rate is at its maximum, shame, embarrassment, hate and un-forgiveness are standard experiences. Let us decide on the set of rule, by which we want to be governed, (therefore if one decides to stay on the outside, then that one would be living dangerously)

There is a typical example of the city of Jerusalem which had twelve gates for the control of its citizens; the traders went out at 06am. When the gates were opened, and returned before 06pm. at which point the gates were shut. It went both ways traders went out and traders came in, interestingly according to **Nehemiah 07:03-4** any citizen disobeyed the city's rule and came in after the gates were shut would be on their own and at their own risk. The city's guards were instructed to protect those within their borders, similarly those persons who decide to experiment outside the realms of God's kingdom rules, stands in jeopardy of great danger. Let this message be a stern warning for kingdom risk takers, let us brake up our folly ground and sow only seeds of righteousness.

No.	Types of Gates	References	Comments
1.	Fish Gate	Nehemiah 03:03,12:39	
2.	Sheep Gate	Nehemiah 12:39	
3.	Horse Gate	Nehemiah 03:28	
4.	Valley Gate	Nehemiah 03:13	
5.	Dung Gate	Nehemiah 03:13,15	
6.	Fountain Gate	Nehemiah 03:15,12:37	
7.	Water Gate	Nehemiah 03:26,12:37	
8.	East Gate	Nehemiah 03:29	
9.	Inspection Gate	Nehemiah 03:31	
10.	Old Gate	Nehemiah 12:39	
11.	Ephraim Gate	Nehemiah 12:39	
12.	Prison Gate	Nehemiah 12:39	

Conclusion

Rules are everywhere: An article is written and published by the WMB department of COGOP (now: Mission Encounter) from the General office carried an article found in a: Baking Power Tin and was wired to an old water pump that was found in a trail across Death Valley in California, in June 1967, and it reads: This pump is all right and will be valid until June 1972, but I have buried a bottle of water under the white rock beside it, and placed it with the cork turned up. There is enough water in it, to prime it and make the washer supple, because by then it will be crystallized, it will be enough but not if you drink it first, so pour a quarter of the water into the pump to soak the leather washer, then pour the rest in the pump and then pump water like crazy, this well has never run dry, So, refill the bottle and put it back, just like you found it, then leave it for the next fellow, all this will only be possible if you don't drink the water first,

So, prime the pump first, follow the instructions, and you can drink all you can for the rest of your life. You will get all you can hold.

This is a lesson for all of us that the person who serviced and operated the pump over the years had the experience, so as smart as we are, experience is greater than just being smart most of the time, so will follow the rules and get it right, and if we don't follow the instructions and out leader, we may just find ourselves outside of God's mercies and have to settle for his judgment. Let's play it by the rules and play it safe.

Chapter 10
How To Treat An Elder (Even When Faulted)

Read 1st. Timothy 05:01 Rebuke not an Elder. And refer to: 1st Samuel 24 which speaks clearly of David and King Saul's robe which he should not have cut even though he got the upper hand of him, and how he later paid the consequence for doing it.

St Luke 17: 03 (Quote NIV) If a brother sins, rebuke him, and if he repents forgive him, if he sins seven times in a day, and seven times come back to you and say I repent, forgive him. James 03:01 "A person who teaches has a solemn responsibility; like the physicians and teachers he who should keep the ancient oath in mind: "FIRST DO NO HARM"

To rebuke does not mean to point out every sin we see, it means to bring to the persons attention with the purpose of restoring him or her to God or to fellow humans, and first check your attitude before you speak. Do you love people are you willing to forgive? Unless rebuke is tie to forgiveness, it will not help the sinning person.

1st Samuels 20, It speaks of loyalty (I believe that we are to be loyal to each other, to our covenant, to our Church, to our leaders, but most of all to our God. Jonathan was loyal to his father Saul because he was his father and the king, he was loyal to David his friend, it was the relationship with, and his loyalty to God that guided him through the conflicting demands of his human relationship. A question, do those closest to you know who has your greatest loyalty. We are to be very careful of betrayal.

1st Samuel 23 to 24 Tells us that King Saul and his men pursued David, a little later Saul got tired and reclined in the same cave that David and his men were, but unknown to him was that he was resting in the reach of his pursuers who now had the upper hand of him, David was boosted up by his men to Kill his pursuer Saul David did not but he cut a piece of the King's robe his robe, but he spared his life, later he was rebuked and had to go penitent, because he should not have touched his leader, even though he was pursuing him.

It is never a good thing to rebuke an Elder, rather entreat him, even if he is wrong, utmost carefulness must be upheld for the sake of the office, leaders are to be respected regardless; it is clear her that those who criticize leaders, usually live in the danger zone: let's look a few examples:

According to:

Nos.	References	Persons & situations	Results
1.	Numbers 12	States that Miriam mocked Moses (her brother) because he had a Cushite wife.	She was stricken with leprosy.
2.	Numbers 16	Koran and some followers led the people of Israel to rebel against Moses; their leader.	The earth swallowed them up.
3.	Nehemiah 2, 4, 6.	Samballat and Tobiah spread rumors and lies to stop the building of Jerusalem's walls.	They were frightened and humiliated.
4.	2nd. Samuels 06	Michal (David's wife) despised him because he danced before the lord.	She remained childless.

5.	2nd. Kings 02	The youths mocked Elisha, and laughed at his baldness.	Bears killed them.
6.	Jeremiah 28	Hananiah contradicted Jeremiah's prophecy with false predictions.	She died two months later.
7.	Acts 13	Bar-Jesus a sorcerer lied about Paul, in an attempt to turn the proconsul against him.	He was stricken with blindness.

David's Prayer.

"Oh Sovereign Lord, Surely there is no one like You, and there is no other God but You"

Conclusion

When it is discovered that an elder errs, much prayer is required before a revelation of the error or a report is made, and the scriptural procedure must be followed to the teeth, in order not to endanger one's self. It is the intent of the writer not to hush up any one or to even attempt to cover up the leader's wrongs, rather to avoid the consequences that could be avoided had the right things be done.

We don't have to make needless mistakes, instead we can learn from those made by others. (Like Uzzah, according to: **2nd. Samuel 06:07**)

Leaders are humans just like everyone else, so from time they misjudge, misguide and misdirect therefore those who lead are to pray for them continuously in order that they will be divinely led, because the scripture declares in **Jeremiah 10:23-24** "It is not in man that walketh to direct his steps. Oh lord, correct me with judgment; not in Thine anger, lest Thou bring me to nothing" (Quote from the NIV)

"The steps of a good, man are ordered by the Lord" Let us endeavor to get it right, and keep it right.

Chapter 11
The Hope That The Resurrection Brings

Read Isaiah 53: 04 – 10

From time, to time, even the very hopeful becomes hopeless. If and when this time comes,   the hopeless will need a greater source of power to embrace them. There is a low estate in humanity known as the lowest ebb. Man as a whole will use his ego to hide behind reality, so a man will none disclose his fears and hurts, and sometimes end up in a state of depression. David got to that point once, and had to rebuke himself. He asked, "why art thou cast-down oh my soul, and why art thou disquieted within me"? It is usually at this point that divine help is sought in order to spare man from the worst and those who refuse to do so usually end up at the worst point.

About 712 B.C. there was a prophecy about the world's greatest burden bearer. One who would be despised and rejected of men, a man of sorrow and acquainted with grief would also be persecuted, and that he would be taken from prison, and would make his grave with the rich in his death because he would have done no violence, nor has deceit in his mouth. The scriptures were fulfilled and at this point Jesus was persecuted, lied on, tried, found to be innocent, yet He was sentenced to death by crucifixion. Yes he was buried and stayed in the grave for three days, but the same rejected Christ is much greater than death. In fact He is larger than life! So as the scripture said, as is stated in Acts 13:35: He will not supper His Holy One to see corruption" then clearly along with the process of embalmment he Raised triumphantly on the third day.

Due to the peril being experienced since the last four months a virus which originated in Wuhan China and now has become a pandemic, which has caused a stay-at-home order to be activated. Therefore we should thank God despite the situation we should be thankful to God for social media it has allowed us to worship from home during this difficult period.

While death is defined as a cessation of all vital functions, the resurrection is defined as the: "Rising of one from the grave" or revival after disuse or inactivity". The fact remains that if there is no death, then there can be no resurrection so sometime we find ourselves in some dead situations, from which we need to be resurrected, and we should do so before mortification takes place. So the quicker it is effected the greater the chance of it becoming a reality.

The following persons were resurrected:

- Jairus' daughter. **St. Luke 08:41-42 & St. Mark 5:22-25** the same day.
- The widow's son in Nain. **St. Luke 07:11-17** (seems like within the same day) according the custom of the Jews.
- Lazarus. **St. John 11: 42-44** (V17 4 days)
- Then he raised himself. **St. Matthew 28:01-20** (3 days)

NB. Jesus did not just die, he was killed, then he raised himself on the third day; if we put ourselves on death row morally by way of our behavior, then say: Arise.

- Arise from malice.
- Arise from disobedience (to both civil and divine authorities)
- Arise from disrespect.
- Arise from hatred (you being there for too long)
- Arise from hurting to a life of healing.
- Arise from petty things.

- Arise from laziness.
- Arise from the lust of the flesh.
- Arise from mischief making
- Arise from lying and stealing, to a life of peace and truthfulness.

Jesus Said: "I am the resurrection and the life, he that believeth in me though he dead yet shall he live, and whosoever believeth on me shall never die".

So, as Jesus said to Lazarus: COME FORT and he came forth. I am speaking to some dead situation this morning to: Come forth, not only from death; but to a new life in Jesus Christ. Come forth now, come forth to stay, and say like Lester Lewis: "I shall not die but Live and s declare the words of the lord. Amen, Amen, Amen."

There is hope in the risen Lord today. So, on that authority; I give you hope also.

Hope to the weak ones.

Hope to the backsliders.

More hope to the strong.

The Lord blesses and keeps you, and cause His face to shine upon you and give you His peace.

Chapter 12
Revive Us Again

Read: Nehemiah 04:01 – 02

In 445 B.C. Nehemiah had an encounter with the enemies of the Jewish Church, led by: **San.bal'lat and Tobiah,** who were determined to put an end to the worshipping of the only True God, prior to that they burnt, tour down the walls of Jerusalem, desecrated the temple, caused temple services to cease. And when Nehemiah and the few feeble Jews decided to **revive** the work, he strengthened his opposition and assault on the church. His question was: "What will these feeble Jews do? Will they fortify themselves? Will they revive the stones out of the heap of the rubble which we have burnt?"

The word **Revive** appears **13** times in the English Bible, **11** times in the Old Testament, and **02** times in the New Testament.

To **revive is to:** revitalize,

Purke-up,

Renew.

Bring life into

Restore.

Restart,

Refresh,

Stimulate.

It makes no sense reviving something which is not of much value, or of any value at all. There should be enough weight on it, to make you want to revive a dead thing.

Read: Nehemiah 06:03-6 Samballat's **Insidious** attempt against Nehemiah (sinister, dangerous and subtle)

V2 . They use crafty device to entrap the Jews (let us meet in one of the villages in the plain of O'no. But they thought to do mischief. (That was mischievous, but also crafty)

When persons are aimed at getting us, they will go at length to do so, as Christians we can't be too careful, and dependency on God for divine protection should be ultimate, because there is no mercy, and very little justice in the world. *US. Vice President. Joe Biden* once said: "Hate is never forgotten, it is only hidden"

V4. They sent messages 4 times to Nehemiah

V5. Five times with an open letter

V9. They say their hands shall be weakened from the work, so they would get an opportunity to re-launch their attack, but Nehemiah said: "O God strengthen my hands **(that is revival)**

My Sisters, My young sisters, brothers too, never you rely on your own strength, trust in the Lord with all of your heart, and lean not on your own understanding, but in all your ways acknowledge the Lord and let Him direct your path. While we are asleep, persons will be planning and plotting how to get us, there is a thought: "If I can't catch you in wheeling, then, I will catch you in the gigging"

As Christians we are always on the job, always engaged in a spiritual battle, we can't relax, because the enemies are not relenting, so we should not get careless. A thought (The author unknown)

"If you are expecting the world to be fair to you, because you are fair, you are fooling yourself.

That is like expecting the lion not to eat you, because you didn't eat him."

There are sufficient evidences of dormant or dead things that have been revived. **(1)** In 1st. Kings 17: 19-22 "And the Lord heard the voice of Elisha, concerning the widow's son who died)   The Lord responded to him there when he brought the child back to life. (When he took the dead child out of his mother's arm, stretched himself upon the dead child three times there he was revived."

2. **Read** 2nd Kings 13:21 they were burring a man, and they spied a band of men and they cast the dead man into the sepulcher of Elisha, and when the man was let down his body touched the bones of Elisha and he was revived and he stood up.
3. **Read Psalm 85: 01 – the end, Sp.** V.06 (after a revival, comes rejoicing, and that is what we want)
4. **Psalm 138: 07:** "Though I walk in the midst of trouble, you will **revive** me, you shall stretch forth your hand against the wrath of mine enemies, and your right hand shall save me"
5. **Habakkuk 3:02** "Oh Lord, I have heard your speech, and was afraid, O lord, revive your work in the midst of the years, and in your wrath remember mercy.

Conclusion

When we are revived what do we do? What should we do? Doing the same old, same old; won't get us anywhere and the whole purpose will be defeated.

I take this opportunity to challenge all of us here today, like Nehemiah, let us rise up and build, because the work is great and we just can't come down.

Be confident and say continuously: Lord Revive us and let us stay revived.

God Bless!

Chapter 13
The God Who Answers By Fire; Call On Him!

Read: 1st. Kings18: 21-26, 29, 38-40

1st Kings 18: 19 (The Message) tells us that when the Baal worshippers called from morning to the time of the evening sacrifice and got no answer, the alter was in disarray, because the constant shuffling and reshuffling of the alter. (Have you ever tried to light a fire when the time is cold or the wood is not good? It can be very frustrating) So Elijah had to rebuild the alter because it was in ruins. He used twelve stones, which represent the twelve tribes of Israel, which he did in honour of God. Whatever we do or intend to do, let it be to the glory of God. We can't worship God on the alter of Baal, and expect God to be please, or to answer us. (**Song** "What if God is not pleased with the way we live?" When Elijah built the new alter, he told them to wet it with water, then they wet it again, and drenched both the wood and the meat with water. Oh what great faith, we can boast on our God when we know Him, and like the three Hebrew boys say: "Even if our God does not deliver us we will not bow".

There was a severe drought in Israel for three and a half years, so the brooks dried up, the grass withered, there was no food for the animals and so things were extremely hard, and the spirit of the people was low. *(nothing n-a-a g-w-a-a-n)*

Because God answers by fire, Elijah's faith was heightened so he said. Go to King Ahab, drought broke, time come, it is going to rain. At that time there was not even as much as an over-cast not a cloud in the sky. As a matter of fact he didn't even talk to the Lord about the rain as yet more-so to have an assurance to give to the king. (Do you know Ahab? have you an ever met him? Let me introduce him to you. He was the eighth king of Israel, a very capable leader and military strategist, the most evil king of Israel, he had the most evil and wicked Baal worshipper as his wife, her name was Jezebel, a covetous woman and a murderer, she even killed Naboth to get his garden. And here is Elijah telling her husband to go and eat and drink because there is the sound of thunder. (Do you know how many times he heard thunder and there was no rain) **Read Vs. 38-45.** However the king complied, now Elijah started to panic because at the point where he told the King it was going to rain he had no evidence of rain. **V.42; "He bowed low, put his head between his knees and cried to the Lord, at that point when he sent his servant to look toward the sea, and there was nothing" C**an you imagine he said to him go again" look again, Elijah had to cry to God like how the Baal Worshippers cried to their gods; The difference is Elijah got answer, and they did not.

According to the Holy Scriptures, all the disciples of Jesus faced opposition as they followed Him. So, whatever we do in His service must be done with full dependence on God for protection and guidance, we should not let opposition and discouragement prevent us from following   the Lord

Fire was used frequently to prove God's goodness toward His people; mention is made in scriptures **515** times, **436** times in the Old Testament and **79** times in the new, in a range of activities as follows:

1.   Fire purifies. Leviticus 01:13
2.   It purges. Exodus 32:20
3.   It destroys. Matthews 03:10
4.   It preserves. Leviticus 03:11
5.   It protects. Exodus 14:22
6.   It draws our attention to God when we are hesitant. Exodus 03:02

7. It gives warmth when it is cold. Exodus 13:22
8. And give light when it is dark. Exodus 13:21
9. It brings an end to hindrances. Matthew 18:18
10. It brings an end to bareness. Matthew 07:19
11. It gives comfort. Matthew 03:11
12. It protects and avenges the enemy. Romans 12:20
13. It illuminates the believers. Acts 02:03
14. It torments the enemy. Revelation 14:10
15. It burns out wrongdoers from among the righteous. Genesis 19:24

The **Chapter 19** account states that after Elijah did so many outstanding things and proved God in so many outstanding ways, he went into depression and wanted to give up, because Jezebel threatened him. Elijah never knew that they were talking him! Ahab told Jezebel about the great thing that Elijah did, and through jealousy she decided to kill him. **Vs. 5 & 6** states that: "God sends angels to prepare meals for you, so rise up, eat," because there is someone who cares for you, but the angel had to come a second time to get him up to speed again, We sometimes have to pluck courage and thread out the enemy, and note carefully that, it is not over until it is over (and declare FIRE! To the enemy)

According to Dr. Charles Stanley (The renown teacher and counselor) When you go to the wrong sources, it is going to be impossible to get the right answers. He being an authority on the subject, imparted to his listeners and his readers that: "before one applies to, or for professional advice, one needs to do extensive checks on the background of the persons who offer such services. Similarly, we should not go to the natural man, for counseling for a spiritual problem, hence one will only get the wrong diagnosis and if the diagnosis is wrong so will be the medicine. (My word: "people cannot deliver what they don't have or more than they have") Some people like Jonah, he had only one message: "Yet in forty days and Nineveh shall be overthrown." **Chapter 03:04** that was his mission and it was well accomplished. So, because of his limited, yet effective mission he was classified as a Minor Prophet.

Jonah's mission was effective although the result was short lived he prophesied between 785 – 760 B.C. interestingly, he prophesied to one of Israel's most powerful kings Jeroboam. The city of Nineveh had a population of more than 120,000 people, but they could not tell their right different from their left **(Jonah 04:11)** so even though God delivered them in 112 years time they were destroyed again. This is saying that God can, and will use whosoever He will, because sometimes we behave as though everything depends on us. God can raise people from whichever state they are in and equip them to do his work. He certainly can make something out of nothing, and do what no other powers can do.

Sometimes we tend to go far away for help, when the available and perfect help and resources are just like eighteen inches away from us, or, just a prayer away. The song suggests: "Oh what peace we often forfeit, oh, what needless pains we bear all because we do not carry everything to God in prayer. It is better to pray than to fret, better to knock because it shall be open to us; or seek and we shall find, because God is never too far away from us.

Chapter 14
Taking Stock Of The Temple, Which Temple Are You?

Reading: 1st. Corinthians 03: 16-17. "Know you not that ye are the temple of God, and that the Spirit of God dwelleth in you? If any man defile the temple of God, him shall God destroy, for the temple of God is holy, which temple ye are. (KJV.)

1st. Corinthians 06: 20. "For you are bought with a price. Therefore glorify God in your body and in your spirit, which are God's"

A. (The word "Temple" "The flat region of either side of the forehead")

B. It is used interchangeably with the words: "**body**", building and house. It is defined by the American Heritage Dictionary as follows:

1. "A building or place dedicated to the worship or presence of the Deity."
2. Any of three successive buildings in ancient Jerusalem,
3. A Synagogue.
4. A Mormon Church.
5. Something considered being the container of divine presence.
6. The Head Quarters of any certain fraternal orders.
7. A place or Building, serving as a focus of several fraternal of something highly valued, In England the two Inns of the Knight Temples of the Court of London.

When spoken of as a building, as in the case of Paul to the Ephesians as is recorded in **Ephesians 02:20**: "And are built on the foundation of the Apostles and Prophets, Jesus Christ being the chief corner stone." Then he speaks of a unit rather than just a component of a unit, which is indeed essential to a fellowship therefore, we need to reinforce it (because we are members of one body.)

- **2nd. Samuel 07:13** Speaks of Solomon's great temple.
- **St. Matthew 24:01** Refers to Herod's temple, that the disciple showed Jesus (that was before Solomon's, but it was it was destroyed.)
- **1st. Corinthians 03:16** Know ye that your body is the temple of the Lord, and the Spirit of God dwells in you.
- **1st. Corinthians 03: 16** "Do you not know that your body is the temple of the Lord, shall you take it and make it members of a harlot? Certainly not". (**NKJV**)

The EST. Do you not know that your body is a member of Christ's do we make it members of a prostitute?

The NLT. Do you realize that your body is a part of Christ should you take and join it to a prostitute? Never.

The Message: God honours the master's body by raising it from the dead; He'll treat you with the same resurrection power, until then, remember that your bodies were created with the same dignity as the master's body. Would you treat it otherwise? I would hope not! There is more to sex than just skin to skin; it is as much a spiritual mystery as a physical fact, as is written in the scriptures. "two becoming one, sex without commitment and intimacy should be avoided by all, because sexual sins are different from all others, in that we violate the sacredness of our bodies they were made for God-given and God-modeled love. Don't you realize that your body is a sacred place, the place of the Holy Spirit? Don't you see that we can't just live the way we please, squander that which God paid a high price for? The physical part of us is not just a piece of property belonging to the spiritual part of us. God owns the whole works, therefore we are responsible to let people see God, in and through our bodies.

2nd. Timothy 02:21 States: "If any man therefore purges himself from these, he shall be a vessel unto honour; sanctified and meet for the master's use, and prepared unto any good works."

In reference to the **Topic:** "Taking stock of the Temple, which temple are you?"

Stock taking is not only for one to know his or her inventory levels, but more-so to prompt us when to make a re-order, and to prevent us from running out of vital supplies. Also to nudge us when to discard some outdated products in order to preserve one's reputation. Remember, Character grows like mushroom, while fame grows like the oak.

Conclusion

Are we trading outdated stocks?

Are we running out of the good stocks? such as:

1. Love, forgiveness, patience, tolerance, honesty, truthfulness, faithfulness, obedience, power, spirituality. Let us continue to check ourselves regularly, to make sure we are not short of the grace of God, in order to live daily in the will of God and in the end to receive the crown of righteousness which fades not away.

Chapter 15
Awaking The Virtuous And The Weeping Women

Prepared and Presented By: My Wife "Arlene".

I will attempt to address the position of the virtuous women who could also be weeping, in order for me to be able to awake you. I must first be awake, after which I can call others, usually some folks are very hard to awake, you have to shake some persons, and others have to be doused with water; while you have to pinch some on their nose before they can be awaken from their deep sleep.

To be virtuous: "is to have a high moral standard" therefore I am making a distinctive call, my sisters let us put our virtue above our hurt and continue to call on the name of the Lord with sincerity in order to epitomize the virtuous woman mentioned in Proverbs 31:01-31. If we embody that specially woman that the wise man Solomon spoke about, then we will not only rise above, but will live above our hurts according to the Psalmist, as recorded in **Psalm 30:05** "For his anger endureth for a moment; in His favour is life, weeping may endure for a night but joy comes in the morning".

There are some things we must do in order to be like the virtuous woman:

- She was honest
- She worked willingly with her hands, and she went to the last mile for her family.
- She did not give in to too much sleep

- She made sure there were enough oil in her lamp and additional oil in her vessel to make sure that her lamp would not out in the night.

We are to make sure that we maintain a high spiritual standard by:

1. Living up to the stand we take in life
2. Rise above life's billows
3. Depend on God for spiritual sustenance
4. Be steadfast in our focus and avoid distractions
5. Even if our prayers remain unanswered stay focus **(Lamentation 03:08)**
6. Shout when such is in order **(Psalm 47)**
7. Weep if you must, but don't live on weeping **(Psalm 06:08)**
8. Recognize that there will be mixed experiences **(Ecclesiastes 03:04)**

It is important to remember that we are not always able to comprehend with all things, but God certainly will, and in the midst of chaos and tragedy He remains steadfast and is a pillar of strength to all.

Sisters remember, we all have a ministry, and we need to maintain it at the highest level possible; like the woman at the center of this discourse who we seek to epitomize, there are many persons watching us and we need to impact their lives in all the positive ways we can. Be aware that some who are watching us, are persons we may not even know, and sometimes we are not even aware that they are watching us but as the old sayings go: "Example" is a language anyone can read.

We need to ask ourselves these questions.

What example am I? Am I the kind of person whose actions are based on the following?

1. Kindness.

2. Faithfulness
3. Generosity
4. Sympathy
5. Understanding
6. And love?

If our lives fit in with the above traits, then we are not only blessed, but highly favoured, those things can only make us powerful, virtuous and highly productive women of God, and can be a force to reckon with, the church needs women of positive influence, kingdom builders, examples to the believers in love, in spirit, in purity and in virtue. When we rise to those levels we only need to depend on God to continue to order our steps, because we can't even walk without him holding our hands.

God Bless

Chapter 16
Playing The Woman's Role

Prepared and Presented By: My Wife "Arlene".

According to the **Genesis 02:21-22** Account, after the Creator created the Universe and all other creatures, then He made man, in His own likeness and in His own image, but then he saw the incompleteness and dissatisfaction of Adam. It was at that point that He made Eve, and she became the mother of all of humanity. One outstanding thing to be noted here is; that he made man from the dust of the earth, but the woman was taken from the side of the man. (Bone of my bone and flesh of my flesh) Therefore, as women we must maintain the value with which we were created. Not from the dust, but from the man's side (A more refined type of material)

My purpose is not just to be a good house keeper, and to bear children, and I am not just playing the woman's Role, (I am not an actress, one who just carry out a function) I am a purpose, I am valuable, I am attractive, Thank God I am loved and respected by my husband, loved by my children, loved by my siblings, my brethren and all who come in contact with me; because I am lovable and I am valuable.

Women, we must place high value on ourselves, let us think positively, act confidently, strive to be the best we can be, be good wives to our husbands, and maintain a good godly relationship with our husbands, relationships that cannot be easily destroyed, knowing that, with Christ in the vessel with us, we can always smile at the storm. Let us epitomize:

- Rebecca the favoured woman.

- Sarah the princess (The daughter of Asher)
- Rachael the woman of patience, who bore a high price, and was well sort after.
- Deborah the prophetess,
- Ruth the Chase blessing
- Hannah the good mother.
- Miriam the ambitious woman
- The Shunammite, the hospitable woman
- Elizabeth the humble woman
- Lydia the business woman
- Dorcas the Evangelist who was also the benevolent seamstress
- The Virtuous woman mentioned in **Proverb 31** she who stretched out her hands to the poor and the needy.

The ancient world was a MAN'S world, therefore those women who made it to prominence, did it by force and /or by strength of character; Esther as an example she took it by force, and at great risk, another prime example is the group of women from Bethany who accompanied the disciples on missionary journeys, who were among the first to be converted in Europe, including Lydia, as recorded in **Acts 16:13-16. Phe-be** a deaconess. **See: Romans 16:01-04.** Paul set a high standard for the women, especially those who are leaders in the church and /or wives of the leading men. See **1st Peter 03:01-06**

In today's world, only the strong survive, in that we have made it to the Hall of Fame, the Guinness Book of Records, ladies it means that our time has come. We no longer need to take it by force "Thank God" The Church to which we belong, has finally released us. So, in that we are released, let us liberate ourselves mentally, as the late Bob Marley said: "None but ourselves can free our minds."

I challenge you my sisters, in the church, in leadership, and in the ministry, let us not reduce ourselves to mockery, or cheapen ourselves for opportunity, or for wealth, let us value our salvation above and beyond all the things that this life offers, let us look fulsomely in the face of Jesus, until the things of this world grow so strangely dim, in light of the Glory and the Grace of Almighty God. let us value our fellowship more than our friendship, because, in friendship, only few benefits, but in fellowship all benefit, let us be tolerant of each other, even though sometimes we don't see eye to eye on certain points; but as Jesus said: "let us grow together until the day of harvest."

Conclusion

Women, we have a purpose, we have a mission, God gave us a plan, and we have a message. And according to **St. Matthew 28: 18-20,** we are commissioned, and all those who know God must know that we are always to be committed, and to do the work of God with a passion, and an intention to win the lost for Christ. In order for us to be effective in our work in ministry. Remember now, we are mandated to be:

1. Vessels of honour
2. Women of integrity
3. Container of respect
4. Women of power and purpose
5. Live at the altar of prayer
6. Being virtuous women
7. Women of high value
8. Courteous and loyal,
9. Be filled with the anointing of the Holy Spirit,
10. And be surrounded by God's divine protection.

My Sisters and Brothers, I love You Lots!

Sisters; be women of Purpose.

God Bless!

Chapter 17
Setbacks Are Better Than Downfalls

Set back: "Means to be placed further back in space or time, to impede or reverse, relapse, or be placed further backward than you might have been."

Downfall: "A great fall, from prosperity to Ruin."

There was a man who had more than his fair share of both setbacks and downfalls; his name is **Job. H**e was portrayed as a wealthy man, one who was upright in his character but although he loved God so well, he suffered more than any other man has ever suffered. He went for riches to rags. He lost his flock. His possessions, his children, his health and eventually his wife. Yet he refused to curse God even though he was prompted by his wife to do so.

Based on Job's life we learnt that knowing God is better than knowing answers because sometimes we think we have the answers but for some reason we are not able to apply them. So then one has to rely on God to resolve it for us. According to: **Job 02:11-13**   Job's friends could not believe his stories of innocence, because: "Cause and effect" is applied to all peoples. Their experiences and views were that: "good thing happens to good people and bad things happen to bad people. So they decided to assist him by influencing him to admit to whatever wrongs he did that caused him to be sufferings so much. They were so determined they almost influenced Job to accept that he have sinned. (Even though he knew he did not)

When things happen to us or people we know, we have to be careful not to become judgmental, because like Job his sufferings was more than just cause and effects, his condition was more than just a set-back, and more than any ordinary down fall. Some of us sometimes have to be prepared for greater service only after we have been through our sufferings, so that we become a living example, to others by being able to say: I have been there done that; and look at me today I am a living testimony. Sometimes too, our sufferings are just straight attacks from the enemy. This may be so, that others can understand and still maintain their hopes in God, after seeking much help from God without getting the answers we anticipate, and in the time that we expect them, we, most time, tend to God why, or why me?, why now.?

We need to know that: "Pain is not always punishment". According to **St. John 09: 01-04**: When Jesus passed by and saw the man who was blind from birth, and the disciples asked Jesus Saying "Master who did sin, that this man or his parents, that he should be born blind?" Then Jesus answered: "Neither hath this man nor his parents; but that the works of God should be made manifest in him". It is clear here that not all pain or defects are directly sin related. So God can allow things to happen in order for us to be more fulfilled. He may even burn our bushes in order to get our attention like he did with Moses if we are not responding to Him with the urgency that he requires. We are not to do the things of God conveniently, according to **Exodus 03:01-06.**

There are several other similar cases, that are like the case of Moses and the burning bush. let us look at Abraham's experience. According to **Genesis 17:01** Abraham had a name change from Abram to Abraham. A name change speaks clearly to a change of identity and lifestyle, this makes it clear that names not only identifies who we are, and what we are supposed to be (example) the name Christian; meaning we are to be Christ-like; and exhibits only Christ-Like traits. So, the name Abraham means: "Father of the faithful and the father of many nations". This suggests that from that day forward faithfulness becomes a lifestyle for Abraham, as compared to him being Abram earlier. This comes with conditionality: Eg. walk before and be thou perfect. What was not said, is that Abram was not walking uprightly neither was he faithful.

This table shows the true walk of the believers:

A brand New Life	**Romans 06:04** …"Even so we also should walk in the newness of life."
A new faith	**2nd. Corinthians 05:07** "For we walk by faith and not by sight."
New levels of Spirituality	**Galatians 05:16** "This a say then, walk in the spirit and ye shall not fulfill the lust of the flesh"
Consistency	**Ephesians 04:01** "I therefore a prisoner of the Lord, beseech you to walk worthy of the vocation wherewith ye are called."
Love	**Ephesians 05: 02** "And walk in love, as Christ also hath loved us, and hath given himself for us an offering and a sacrifice to God for a sweet-smelling savour."
Caution	**Ephesians 05:15** "Seen then that ye walk circumspectly, not as fools but as wise."
Illumination	**1st. John 01:07** "But if ye walk in the light as ye is in the light, we have fellowship one with another, and the blood of Jesus Christ his son, cleanseth us from all sins."
Christ-like-ness.	**1st. John 02:06** "He that saith, he abideth in Him, ought himself also to walk, even as He walked."
Walk in truth	**Psalm 26:03** "For Thy loving kindness is before mine eyes: and I have walked in Thy truth."
Wait Upon God	**Isaiah 40:31** "But they that wait upon the Lord shall renew their strength; they shall mount up with wings like as eagles, they shall run, and not be weary; and they shall walk, and not faint."

Almost everyone at some point has some setbacks, and during that time one tends to fell cast-down or disquieted, because it may appears as if there is not going to be any way out of that situation. The wise man Solomon said, in **Proverbs 03:01** "To everything there is a season, and a time to purpose under the heavens." So, if and when one finds himself / herself in that situation, be reminded that this too will pass. A down-fall in most case in Scriptures means; to be dead. At that point there is no more hope, but sometimes there are blessings in setbacks because we sometimes escape so snares of the enemy, or we might not be in the position to deal with certain things as a particular time but may be able to do so at other times. So the scripture come alive here in **Jeremiah 10:23** "Oh Lord I know that the way of man is not in himself, it is not in man that walketh, to direct his steps." Therefore we just need to commit our ways unto the Lord and let Him order our steps.

Chapter 18
Maturity Speaks To The Point Of The Christian's Perfection

Scripture Reading, Hebrews 11: 01-06

Hebrews 11:01-06 speaks of some heroes of faith from whom we can learn how to be mature and be like them, or may even be better than they, comparing ourselves with those heroes, the advantage that we have to be better than they, because we can bench mark them, while most of them were initiator or pace setters.

Most successful persons, companies, organizations and countries are successful because they could stay aside and study the behaviors or performances of others, improve on their weaknesses   and were able to become greater than their mentors.

Faith

Hebrews 11:06 "States that without it is impossible to please God."

Ephesians 02: 08 "It is by Grace that we are saved through faith, and not by ourselves" it is that faith that makes us believe that we will sit in heavenly places, because we are now united with Christ and the saints, and will live in power and victory,

Maturity

James 01:04 – 05 Tells us that it is by our patience that our works will be perfected and entire wanting nothing, and if any of us lack wisdom we should ask of God who gives us liberally, in-fact He gives to all who asked.

Philippians 03:15 Speaks to the point to the point of perfection, and further states that it is available and attainable, it is the prize of a higher calling and verse 16 states that we must all walk by the same rule, and mind the same thing.

Ephesians 04: 13 says: "Till we come in the unity of the faith and of the knowledge of the Son of God to a perfect man, unto the measure of the stature of the fullness of Christ."

READ 1st Corinthians 02: 05 – 07   (A deeper faith for the mature)

Christians

Acts 11:26 The believers were first called Christians at Antioch, It was because the believers spent time in Prayer and in the Study of the words, they demonstrated the good Christ-like traits, after they spent one year there, and the citizens saw their works that they were able to compare them to that of Christ, they concluded that, these people are like Christ, it was there and then that they were first called Christians.

Conclusion

In 1St. **Peter 01:05** Peter wrote as one who knew Christ personally, he also knew that following Jesus was not going to be always easy, yet he became fainthearted when Christ was arrested and three time he denied knowing Christ. Later on he wrote to the brethren throughout Asia Minor, don't let persecution or any other trials rob you of the Joy of salvation, because the reward will be great for all those who endure those test, for the praise, glory and honor of Christ's name. And in **verse 13** he wrote: One aspect of our faith and maturity is for us to: "Gird up the lions of your mind, be sober, and rest your hope fully upon the grace of God that is to be brought to you as the revelation of Jesus Christ.

Chapter 19
Safety And Success Through Service

Reading: Psalm 112: 05 "A good man deals graciously and lends, He will guide his affairs with discretion"

Deuteronomy 16:16-17 states "We should give according to our ability. Giving is not just money or service, but also of our talent and our time" and Jacob said **in Genesis 28:22**. "Of all that Thou shall give me I will surely give the tenth unto Thee" (this is separate and apart from one's occupation). If we are called to serve, then the Jacob's experience that we model is separate from our occupation. So we should make time for service to God, to our community and our fellowmen. One doctor said recently on a radio program that: "To continue living on planet earth, then the rent we pay is our service to our fellowmen."

Paul said to the Philippians brethren as is recorded in **Philippians 02:04:** "Look not every man on his own things, but every man also on the things of others". So, he exhorted them to love, unity and service". At this unprecedented time in the world's history when the common term being used is: "The New Norm" here and now we are given an opportunity to perfect our service to God; which is in fact, our service to our fellowmen. So Jesus communicated to his disciples in **St. Matthew 25:31–46** when he gave the **Service Test,** then in **Verse 40** he said: "Verily I say unto you. Inasmuch as ye have done it unto one of the least of these my brethren, ye have done it unto me". This is to say when we love God, in essence we are saying that we love people, and to the contrary when we hate people then it is God that we hate as well.

Looking at the subject at hand, the time suggests that we make concerted efforts to be different by our approach to each other and to kingdom activities and expectations, because some of us, we are Christians alright, but we don't practice giving back at all, we are only concerned about getting, getting, getting. We don't give back to our parents, nor, our siblings, nor to our Church and community, all we are concerned about is, how will it benefit us? The point cannot be overstated, there are the fifteen established Spiritual Disciplines that are practiced by Pentecostals and even though it is looked at by some, with least importance, the facts remain, that service is the most important of them all. A friend of mine was on vacation in the United States of America once but things weren't going well with him then, in his moment of despair he got out of the house and went for a walk, as he past a church gate, he was prompted to go in and ask for prayer, for a change in his circumstances. So, he went to the Priest for blessings, he anticipated that he would be anointed with oil and be prayed for by the priest; but the priest told him: "Do a good deed to a less fortunate person everyday and your success will be guaranteed". That was similar to the rich ruler was told to sell all that he had and give to the poor. However from that day forward my friend took a new approach to life.

There are a few things that we can do differently.

1. Make people feel important.
2. Grow the service attitude to higher heights every day.
3. Make service a rule and always remember that, the support you give to others is the only hurdle between you and what you want to be
4. Serve, Serve, Serve. Even when a risk is involve sometimes.

Acts chapter **10:38-39** The Apostle Peter gave an account of how God anointed Jesus with the power of the Holy Ghost and Power, equipping Him for service; then he went forth doing good and healing those that were oppressed of the devil. Like Jesus, we must take pleasure in serving others, some people bask in the fact of being served by others but never want to be a servan. **Acts 20:35** states: "I have showed you all things, how that so laboring ye ought to support the weak, and to remember the words of the Lord Jesus, how it said. It is more blessed to give than to receive" So then the real blessing that is associated with service, is not to be at the receiving end. Clearly note here that service and serving are two tests that we continue to fail, because some of us always only want, want, want; rather than to give, give, give.

In the recent past I reiterated the point that sometimes there is a set of persons who, when a call is made for money even for a very good cause, they may not have the money to give to the call, so we could sometimes give service instead, toward the said call, however they don't even give service either, so they will always remain at the lower end of the socio-economic ladder. With the sowing and reaping model, what can we do differently, what will we do differently.

I will seek to benchmark Samuel in his youthful days, at a point when he did not yet know the lord. According to **1ˢᵗ Samuels 03:01-21.** Service is a good trait for youths to take on. Samuel became the last of the Judges in Israel and formed the transitional link between the Eras of the Judges and the Kings. He served Eli at a time when he was laid down and his eyes went dim. V.02. For him, who did not yet know the Lord, yet he demonstrated the right attitude of a servant; it played well in his favour and paid a high dividend. It was while he was serving Eli in the absence of his (Eli's) two sons: Hoph'ni and Phin'e-has whose reports were very bad. At the time when the Lord called Samuel he was so inexperienced he could not even recognized the voice, or the call of the God, neither did he know that God knew his name; moreso to have called him. But Eli guided him and aided him in answering the call.

Conclusion

From time to time we impress others by our expressions that are not truly in harmony with who we truly are. In that case we would have deceived ourselves and may be deceived others, but we should seek to be true representative of Christ, and that should rightfully be so by:

- Our actions
- Our speaking
- Our behavior
- And by our business principles

We should all pledge today to grow the service attitude first (which is giving, giving, giving.) and always remember that our success and safety depends on our service to our fellowmen; Brethren it is important that we learn to love people. Like Jesus does, which is done by practicing, practicing, practicing, until we learn how to be genuine.

God bless you all as we take on this one, "Safety and success through service" as one of the NEW NORMS.

Chapter 20
Renewed & Restored For A Brighter Tomorrow

Scriptures:

2nd. Chronicles 15: 07 – 15 (V.8 "The renewing of the Alter of the Lord" V.13 (whosesoever was guilty of Prayerlessness was put to death whether they were: men, women or Children. It is quite evident that there is always a better way to do things. In the event of King Asa's reign in Jerusalem, he along with his contemporaries: Azariah, Baasha, Hanani, Ben-Hadad and Zerah, they realized that the same old same old tatics would not give them the War-victory they anticipated so they reformed the Alter of the Lord, by repairing it; and although it was established that the army of the Cushites (his enemies) was much larger and stronger than his, with that in mind before they met in the Valley of Zephathah; Asa prayed to God to enable them and for sure the Cushites were defeated. (Victory through Prayer and dependency on God)

Psalm 103: 01 – 22 (Vs. 4&5 Speaks of the renewing of the youth like the eagles. It is said in the story of the eagle's renewal; (That they can renew their lives by: biting off their feathers, talons and beaks and then re-grow them and may add to their lives up to 10 more years, I later learn that is not true, because when the Eagles naturally deteriorates then they could not survive for five months but the experts said the birds would die during that period. Having no flight feathers, beak or claws, they would be unable to find food and survive from the cold, so death would be eminent.

What the amplified Bible said is that. David was saying: as the eagles go   through the different stages of life, new feathers are graciously provided by the Creator, similarly those who constantly seek to restore themselves, will grow naturally, and be strong like the eagles and be able to soar high like them too. So the benefits of renewal are very special, and are compared with that of an extra- ordinary bird, the eagle. (Their life span is 20 -30 years but they can live up to 70 years depending on the care they received and the habitat they are in.

Ephesians 04:14 – 25 (Vs. 22 -25 speaks of a renewed life)

Every living entity has to be renewed at some point or the other, whether seasonally or after reproduction, especially in the case of the females. At which point assessments are done and new goal set for the upcoming period. Usually the assessments give an idea of where and how adjustments should be made for improvement, and if there are aspects of performance in the previous term, that was not effective enough, then sometimes certain segments would be either modified or discontinued; in the case of equipment they must be serviced periodically and parts renewed in order to optimize performance and reduce down time .

Just as certain members of the human body continue to grow: such as the hair and the nails just to mention a few, the Bible states in **Colossians 03:08-10:** "But you must rid yourselves of all such things as these; anger, rage, malice, slander, and filthy language from your lips. Do not lie to each other, since you have taken off your old self with its practices, and have put on the new self, which is being renewed in the image of its Creator." In other words we have outgrown those old habits, so, the energies are now to be concentrated on renewal and not by carrying the old thing of the past, rather let us do everything to avoid conflict in our families, and in the church, because our conduct should match our faith in God.

Christian renewal means that rather than just making resolutions and just having good intentions, we must take the right actions and focus on them like putting on our clothes. Every Christian is on a continuing education program which is aimed at knowing and being more like Christ every day, it is a lifelong learning, with an aim to find the rich treasures that are in Him so that we will be able to enrich others, and be enriched by them, as together we keep in line with Him. These are some of the renewed knowledge, to enable us to remain in the image of the Creator Himself, and we should always be seeking for more.

Conclusion

Many of us have started our Christian journey on excellent footings, but as time goes by we have somehow drifted from the path of excellence; and are really in need not just for renewal but also for restoration

Renewal is: a rebirth, amendment, recompense and rekindling of standards.

Restoration is: A return, renovation, renewal, restoration, or reimbursement of something that has lost its originality; this is to mean that along life pathway we will all need to be rekindled and renewed in order to be in good stead with Jesus Christ. So then let us all practice renewal consistently.

God Bless

Chapter 21
Being Contented In The Place Of Refuge

Scripture Reading: Psalm 46: 1-11

V.01 "God is our refuge and strength, a very present help in trouble"

V.11 "The Lord of host is with us; the God of Jacob is our refuge"

Refuge: Is a shelter from pursuits or danger, or trouble (A city of refuge for those guilty of manslaughter in ancient Israel, a house or institution for the homeless persons, to give shelter or, is resorted to in difficulties or distress.) The Bible named **six cities** as being cities of refuge: *Golan, Ramoth, and Bosor, on the East of the Jordan River, and Kedesh, Shechem, and Hebron on the Western side.* According to **Joshua 21:01-45**, but in **V33** it is said that the cities and suburbs combined were thirteen in all, and it is mentioned again **V41** in that when combined the cities of the Levites with the other tribes of Israel then it forty-eight cities in total.

The cities of refuge were set aside so that even when the worst of crimes were committed (unintentionally) once the offenders reached the city's gate before being apprehended by their pursuers they would be shielded by the elders and the guards at the City of refuge, in addition to that the offender would remain in safety until the Elders make a ruling.

Abner the son of Ner was the captain of Saul's great army (Ner was Saul's uncle) so they were close relatives; (first cousins.) There were some arguments and mix-up with Abner and Saul's concubine by the name of Rizpah. So, Ish-Bosheth the ruler in Saul's kingdom said to

Abner: "Why has thou slept with my father's concubine? (Your former boss) he was wroth, at that time, their mission was to unite in the battle against the Philistines, Abner was inside the City of refuge because he slew Asahel the brother of Joab and Abishia in the battle at Gibeon; Isa-hel was persuing Abner in battle Abner warned him to stop persuing him and that he did several times so Abner killed him. 2nd. **Samuels 03:27-30** records as follows: "Then Joab took Abner aside, inside the city's gate to speak with him quietly, and there he stabbed him under his fifth rib and there he died (as a revenge for his brother's death) 2nd. Samuels 03:33 states that **"Abner died a fool's death"** So, they buried Abner in Hebron.

It is quite clear here that all wrongs done in secret will some day come to light, Abner did not know that his secret acts would one day come to light, and in those days whenever a servant sleeps with the kings partner, it meant he intends to take the kings throne as well. So Ish-Bosheth being the Ruler in the kingdom realized that his position was at stake, but he was afraid of Abner, because he was a very high profiled army general. Once a person was placed in the city of refuge, then one would be free if the Ruling King dies; or when the Elders of the land would have tried you and found you innocent, then one would be freed to returned to his family and their homeland.

Contented: To be contented is to be satisfied, pleased, happy, content, comfortable, relaxed or at ease, here we see an extra ordinary army general like Abner, (heights of great men both reached and kept; one who ruled under two great kings: Saul and Ish-Bosheth, Abner was a smart and witty general and should have known better not to bargain with someone from the opposing side, especially when two factions are engaged in the heights of a conflict. Beside for someone military and has ascended to the level of an army general, he should not have died a fool's death. Because we cannot underestimate the capabilities of the enemy, nor ever let down our guards; beside, once you are in a place of refuge, you should be contented, even if you are not happy, one thing is sure; and that is, that you would be safe' don't step aside with anyone, the risk is much too high you should not trade your safety for any indefinite bargain.

One of life's greatest lesson learnt, is that there can be contentment without safety, Abner obviously relied on his own capabilities and reputation, but the wise man Solomon said in **Proverbs 03:07**: "Be not wise in thine own eyes, fear the Lord, and depart from evil." **Proverbs 26:12** records: "Seest thou a man wise in his own conceit, there is more hope of a fool than of him" While **1ˢᵗ. Corinthians 08:02** puts it this way: "If any man think that he knoweth anything, he knoweth nothing yet as he ought to know" therefore we dare not trust our own selves, because we have seen the failures of many, especially that of Abner. He was feared by many even the very powerful and the renown, yet because of the human limitation he did not anticipate dying a fool's death, on the other hand the scripture says: Whose shedeth man's blood, by man shall his blood will be shed, for in the image of God made He man" So even we feel secure by our own skill and perceives defence. It comes to prove that there is no safety or contentment outside of the will of God.

The lessons learnt from the death of Abner, can be categorized as being superlative in nature and an experience that can take us through life. According to **Psalm 46:01** "God is our refuge and strength, a very present help in trouble" those of us who find refuge in Jesus Christ, should know that where safety is concern; in Jesus we have it all! The difference is to risk our lives, by stepping away from the place of Safety, is a risk too high, therefore all those who have not yet found refuge in Jesus Christ, or those overtaken by the pursuers before they reach the city of refuge is at great risk, mark whatever was not done by Abner cannot be done again. (At death, task left undone will remain that way, and as the good song say: "I don't want to leave behind an unfinished task." Therefore let's not put off for tomorrow, what we can do today; (don't procrastinate) but make sure the application is towards the right things. I will inject the following thought:

- If it is not right, don't do it,
- If it is not true don't say it
- If you are unsure, don't risk it.

Conclusion

Safety and contentment are things good people deserve; it is said good things happen to good people, and bad things happen to bad people, however to the contrary things sometimes work against even nature itself, In that we don't know for sure, if life will always be kind to us, then let us put our lives in the hands of the One who is greater than life.

Ephesians 05:15-16 "See then that ye walk circumspectly, not as fools, but as wise. Redeeming the time, because the days are evil" the Redemption Song book says: "Christians, seek not yet repose; hear the guardian angel say, Thou art in the midst of foes; Watch and pray." So, the only solid Rock on which one can stand, is on Christ, the proven one, for all other grounds are but sinking sand. "Let us make every effort to make our faith bigger than our fears, because perfect love casteth out all fears, and where there is love there is life, where there is life, there is hope, and where there is faith, miracles happen, where there is peace, there is God, and when you have God, You have everything."

Chapter 22
Desiring God, Like The Hart Pants After The Water Brooks

Read Psalm 42:01-02 "Speaks of the hart and the water brooks and how the Soul of the Psalmist (one of the chief musicians, who was a son of Korah. Korah was a Levite who lead a rebellion against Moses, according to Numbers 16:01-35, he should be doing temple service but he lead a rebellion instead, so God instructed Moses and Aaron; according to Vs. 20 & 22 to separate themselves from among the congregation so that He could consume them, and they would be spared. V.30-35 States that the earth opened and swallowed them up with all their possessions) he pants after God" (a spiritual thirst for God to help him out of his troubles according to V.3 states the he was in disappointment and grief.) So, it was not in the normal self driven search for God, or an effort of voluntary praise to God or adoration as it should be it was a situation where his back was against the wall, and there was no other way out or available help he was experiencing prolonged grief, after the death of his father along with his contemporaries, to that extent that his very countenance became sick and unwelcoming. His plea concludes in V.11 where he again asked his soul: "And why are you disquieted within me?" So after he reprimanded himself while wearing a sick countenance for far too long, eventually he said: Hope in God, for I shall yet praise Him, the health of my countenance and my God"

Even though Korah and his contemporaries were swallowed up by the ground his descendants remained faithful to God, but their worship and the playing of the music in the temple became a tradition but had no dedication, no commitment hence no harmony, no joy, not much meaning he was still in utmost grief. Had he not known the joy and blessings that true worship give, then he would not pant after God the way he did, but he knew full well what was missing from the life; The Life Application Bible puts it this way: "As the life of the deer depends upon water, so our lives depend upon God, those who seek Him and long to understand Him find never-ending life, that is the reason why the Psalmist would not rest until he restored his relationship with God, because he knew that his entire life depended on it.

The Hart: Is a European male deer over four years old, red in colour, is among the clean edible animals, it can drink up to one gallon of water per day, at a size of 100 lbs so that can be factorized depending on the size of the animal. Its life depends on it, so It runs as fast as 46 MPH (The distance between Mandeville, Manchester and Spanish Town, St. Catherine when it runs and pants it drips the water from its body, the faster it runs the more it pants, the more it pants the greater the risks of collapsing, due to dehydration it is searching for the water brooks, the more desperate it gets the faster it runs, but the need to find the water brook (The source of survival) supersedes the very need of the water lost.

Why would a deer pant? **Panting is** how some animals cool when overheated. **Deer have** very few sweat glands, which we use to exchange heat, **panting is** the mechanism that is used in place for cooling in the place of sweat glands. Quenching the thirst is not the only purpose it pants, but finding the water brook and submerging its feet in the brook also erases the scent trail, So, when the scent trail is broken, it's pursuers can no longer follow him because the animal's tracking feature is deactivated, by the feet washing exercise, that gives the hart an opportunity to evade it's pursuer. Note though that the more the hart runs, the greater the risk of making other harts loosing track of them. So for us who runs hard after God no wonder the enemies can't find us; we all have enemies don't we? knowingly or unknowingly, people pursue us for one thing or another, this is one way of making our enemies our footstool, those of us who are listening to me today (or reading this discourse) will know that the best way to evade the enemy is to pursue hard after God. (The song hide me oh my Saviour hide till the storm of life is past;" or, "Lord I am running after You." Let us go harder after God because, the harder we go after Him is the better the outcome will be.

While the **psalm** is attributed to the "sons of Korah", the text is written in the first person singular. ... The psalmist bemoans all the troubles he has endured in his exile and prays for salvation. He laments his remoteness from the temple of God and expresses his desire for the renewal of the divine presence.

Why does a deer pant after water?

Panting is how some animals cool when overheated. **Deer** have very few sweat glands, which we use to exchange heat, panting is their mechanism, place of the cooling more sweat glands offer.

Do deer pant like dogs?

Just **like dogs**. **Deer** cant sweat, the only way they can sweat is through the mouth, nose, maybe the hooves I'm not sure; just **like dogs**. Actually, **deer** CAN sweat, so he was probably just breathing hard and not **"panting"** to cool itself through evaporation **like** a **dog**. (Pushing off the body heat through the mouth and the hooves)

Opinions vary, but most experts suggest that whitetails deer weighing approximately 100 pounds in body weight, will need about 2 to 3 quarts of **water** per **day,** apparently, and that should be factorized base on the size and weight of the animal; the **water** needs increase in hot and dry weather, probably because of panting, and small increases in skin **water** loss.

Those of us who are God chasers, stands in good stead of finding total protection in God, because He hedge us around, and shelter us like the hens shelter their chicken, therefore there is no fear, because perfect love casteth out all fears. Let's go forward for God, keep our eyes on Jesus. Look fully in His wonderful face and let the things of this world grow strangely dim in light of His glory and Grace.

Section 2
To Established And Potential Leaders

Chapter 23
Fulfilling The Call Of God On Your Life

Read: Isaiah 45: 21-22 (A Universal Call)

1st. Samuels 03:01 – 10 (Samuels Call) an individual one

SAMUEL: The son of Elkanah and Hannah. He was the last of the Judges of Israel, while (Saul was the first King of Israel) a very serious transition

> **Verse 04** shows the first Call he got
>
> **Verse 06** he was called the 2nd time
>
> **Verse 08** he was called the 3rd. time
>
> **Verse 10** he was called the 4th. time, (it a rept. call)

The point about the fourth call is that his name was called **twice** this is significant and of a serious nature.

However according to verses **1&2** Samuel was still a child and he did not yet know the Lord, and there were no open vision, so Samuel was as it were ignorant and unfamiliar with the voice of an unknown and unseen person. Beside the word of God was not yet openly declared in his presence, and according to the current situation with Eli and his sons. His thought process and his listening ears were more or less attuned to Eli call.

At that time Eli's two boys: Hopni and Phinehas behaved badly and lost the favors of God and because they were no longer in harmony with their father who was now an old man, althought both were priest **(1ˢᵗ Samuel 02: 22-25)**

The two sons were now missing in action regarding home duties so Samuel capitalized on filling the gap that they should fill at home it is said that Samuel got a bed and place near to Eli's room so that he could hear his calls and be able to attend to him, he focused on Eli so much that even God was calling him, his only expectation was Eli.

1. He was too young to know
2. Where ones treasurers are there will his heart be also
3. Although Eli lost favor and relationship he still had experience and was still vested with the appointment (that comes with favors)
4. He was able to hear but wasn't able to distinguish.
5. You need to know God' voice
6. We must be careful not to run to the wrong sources
7. We need to stay close to our source and be able to indentify unfamiliar voices.

It is important to respond to our calls, because we sometimes a don't know, we may not know what plans other persons have for us, Samuel didn't fully understand his mother Hannah's pledge, but she pledged him as gift to God before he was conceived in her womb, then where was he? Neither did he knew the process his poor mother went through before he was conceive

Hannah was fervent in worship, and effective in prayer, and although she struggle with a sense of self-worth because she did not conceive at the time when Elkanah wanted her to bear children, and her contender Peninnah mocked her and called her barren, **READ Chapter 1: (V9) &26-28**

Elkanah loved her unconditionally but she constantly responded to the mocks and jeers of Peninnah and eroded her self-worth. (We need to stop listening to those people with their Peninnah spirit, (who a badmouth you and a wash their negative-ness) on you, because you know that Jesus loves you.

I will focus on six outstanding persons who like Samuel received divine calls, at which points they change their conditions, and fulfilled the callings on their lives.

1. In **Exodus 12:01 Abraham** was told to "get out of his country and from his kindred and from his father's house, to a la that God would show him".

2. To: **Moses** God said as recorded in **Exodus 03:10.** "Come now therefore, and I will send you to Pharaoh, that you may bring forth my people; the children of Israel out of Egypt".

3. **Gideon:** The Lord said to him: "Go in your might and you shall save Israel from the hands of the Midianites, have I not send you? **Judges 06: 14.**

4. **Elisha**, the son of Shaphat who was plowing with twelve yokes of oxen before him,   and he said to Elijah and the twelve as they passed by him: Cast your mantle upon him. **1ˢᵗ· Kings 19:19**

5. **Isaiah 06:08** States: "And I heard the voice of the Lord saying who shall I send and who will go for us? Then said I. "Here am I, send me". See also Jeremiah **01:02.**

6. **Paul** said as recorded in **Acts 26:16:** Rise up stand upon your feet, for I have appeared unto you for this purpose, to make you a minister and a witness both of these things which you have seen and those which I will reveal unto you.

Conclusion

Those six examples of the call of God on person's lives are outstanding in nature, and clearly demonstrate the different stages of a divine call.

> (1) God does the calling,
> (2) The individual knows that he or she is called and
> (3) His or her superior identify the call

Is our call fulfilled?

God Bless.

Chapter 24
When Good Followers Become Leaders

Scripture Reading: Psalm 05:08 "Lead me oh Lord in thy righteousness, because of mine enemies, make Thy way straight before my face."

It is clear that in some circles everybody wants to lead, but if there are no followers then, there is no need for leaders. Good leaders are usually those persons who are called, and not necessarily those who have leadership thrust upon them, nor those who inherit it through family line. There are other types of leaders as well, some were born leaders, some inherit it, and while others have it trusted on them. Among them all, are the good followers who are God Called to the position of leadership in the Church. It is expected of us to differentiate ourselves from secular leaders in society in that a Christian leader has to uphold the God Called sanction for continuity and success.

The 10 types of leadership styles are:

1. Autocratic
2. Democratic
3. Laissez-faire
4. Coaching
5. Transformational
6. Charismatic
7. Bureaucratic
8. Visionary
9. Pacesetter
10. Servant

For the purpose of compatibility with Church life and Church Administration I will choose Style #10 "Servant leadership" and give credits to Cheryl Bachelder (Servant Leader Extraordinaire) who shared her company's performance and successes over a ten year period (Popeyes Louisiana Kitchen)

Business success takes time, likewise Church success takes time like every other business entity, patience with diligence can do great things. While we can't win people into the Kingdom we can win them to the Church, God promised to do the Kingdom drawing. (Our duty is to continue to lift up Jesus) When Cheryl Bachelder took over her now coveted company in 2007 the company's profit trends were negative, but in seven years time sales were up by 25% and profit was up by 40%. Then in ten years time that company became the benchmarked company.

Some of the business principles that led to her success were: patience, effective communicating skills, self confidence, ambition, high energy, strong multitasking skills and the ability to motivate others, these are some good traits that Church leaders can adopt. In order to be successful leaders, let us be good followers, follow the good examples only, with full dependency upon the Holy Spirit; and say continually "I can do all things through Christ that strengthens me." When God made the covenant with Abraham according to the Sunday School lesson of May 03, 2020 with reference to **Galatians 03:15** it took 430 years before the Law was given to the people.

The mentality of some people and even some organizations is: "I need it now" urgency is good but is not always the best. When God gave Abraham the promise to bless him and to multiply his seed he and his wife Sarah got inpatient and got in trouble.

Followers: Followers are those who subscribe to the teachings or methods of others, servants, attendants, or subordinates.

Leaders: Leaders are those who lead or guide, those in charge or in command of others, the head of the political parties, or organizations, those who have influence or power, especially those of a political nature, the principal performer of a band.

The words followers and leaders are two words that are not used frequently in the English Bible. In my research of the word: **"Follower"** is only found **eight** times in the New Testament, and is not mentioned in the Old Testament. When looked at other parts of speech I found **13** in total in the New Testament and **02** in the Old Testament. The word "**Leader**" even with the different parts of speech was only found **twelve** times, **nine** times in the Old Testament and **three** times in the New Testament.

Words	Part of Speech	Scriptures	Comments
Follower	Is a Noun	Philippians 03:17 1st. Peter 03:17 Ephesians 05:01 Hebrews 06:12 1st. Peter 03:13	The following benefits are the blessings for the followers of the true leaders. they are: (1) Spiritual knowledge (2) Spiritual Light (3) Guidance of the still small voice. (4) Heavenly Honor. (5) Divine Example.
Following	Is an Adjective	2nd. Peter 02:15	Those followers who forsake the right way and are following the ways and enticements of Balaam they are

			sure to reap the wages of unrighteousness.
Followeth	Verb	Hosea 06:03 Psalm 63:08 St. Mark 09:38 St. Luke 09:49 St. John 08:12 St. John 10:27 Ephesians 05:01 1st. Peter 02:21 Revelation 14:04	Clearly those who follow on to know the Lord shall receive blessings that are liken unto the former rain, the latter rain and the rain. David said my soul followeth hard after Thee, Thy right hand upholdeth me. John the disciple asked Jesus: "How can one who does not follow us, cast out devils in Your name?" But Jesus told him, give him a chance, he is not really against us. Jesus is the light of the world; he that followeth after Him shall not walk in darkness, but shall have the light of life. My sheep hear my voice, and I know them, and they follow me, and I give unto them eternal life. Jesus gave us examples for us to follow, if we do, we can and will become good leaders. For the

			best leaders ever, are those who are willing to follow others.

Words	Part of Speech	Scriptures	Comments
Lead	Can be used as a Verb, a Noun, and an Adjective. Example. **(1)** As a lead man, a lead horse, or a lead singer. **(2)** By taking the lead, being in the front.	Deuteronomy 32:12 Psalm 05: 08 Psalm 25:05 Psalm 31:03 Psalm 139:10 St. Matthew 15:14 St. Luke 06:39	States that the Lord is the only God, there were no strange gods in the midst, and David said: "Lead me oh Lord in thy truth, teach me, I will wait on You, for You are the God of my salvation. Thy right hand shall lead me Thy right hand shall hold me." Jesus taught the people; in a parable. Beware of false leaders they are like blind leading blind, and both will fall into the ditch
Leader	Noun	Isaiah 09:16 Isaiah 55:04	Isaiah warned against False Leaders who mislead the people and caused them to be destroyed,

			the lord has no pleasure in those leaders. For the Lord has given them to the people as leaders and commanders.
Leadeth	Verb	Psalm 23:02 – 03 Isaiah 48:1 St. John 10:03	Just like a shepherd leads his sheep, that is by going in front, and by leading them to be refreshed, to be protected and in the path of righteousness. And teaches them. And when necessary he personalizes his treatment by calling them by their names.
Leading	Adjective	None	Those who initiated, by going in front.
Leadership	Noun	None	However the Priest, the Levites the Elders, the Ministers and the Patriarchs, they were the leadership of the early Church.

There is the importance of getting the best types of leadership Training for effective leadership. It has been proven that temperament and styles have a lot to do with the effectiveness of one's leadership, regardless of the extent of leadership training received. It also has to do with the work culture in the region where you lead; the culture of the people you are leading, along with the culture of the person in the top leadership of the organization in which you are employed. A combination of all those points should be taken into consideration in order to have harmony in the organization where you are employed. A good Team Spirit is usually an asset to productive leadership. A spiritual leader usually depends on God for divine direction because "the only way one can be good is when his or her steps are ordered by God" (**Jeremiah 10: 23-24**. Matthew Henry's commentary.) Let's not forget that the sowing and reaping scenario usually plays a significant role in outcomes.

Leading With Pride

There are the special occasions where one has got to lead persons who are older than him or her; that leader need to be firm yet respectful. To be respectful does not mean that you shirk your leadership responsibilities. Be kind but not stupid. Leaders should always set goals that are aligned with time limits. Church leadership has administration as a part of its responsibility, while at other levels of the same organization there may be persons in top leadership whose responsibility in strictly administrative.

It must be clearly noted that job descriptions should be made available for all levels of the organization in order that each person performs within his or her own boundaries to avoid overlapping is duties which could cause confusion and or chaos. If every leader remains good followers, then they too will be followed and there will be more success and harmony in the organizations especially within the religious organizations.

Chapter 25
Living In Obedience To God's Word

Read Joshua 01:06-09

Obedience: is, submission to another's will,

Joshua succeeded Moses as leader for the children of Israel in 1451 B.C., leading them from the land of Egypt journeying to the land of Canaan. He was a leader and commander of the children of Israel. The NIV puts it this way: "Joshua was an example of an excellent leader; he displayed full confidence in the strength of the Lord, and great courage in the face of opposition and was always willing to seek God's direction.

1st. Timothy 06:12 NIV "Fight the good fight of faith and make it a profession" because the price of success is paid through obedience to God's words, and is clearly mapped out in the scriptures as the strait was to success. The victory against **A'I.** could not be realized without obedience to God. Clearly they lost it the first time, because one man (Achan) brought defeat to the entire nation of Israel when he stole the Babylonian garment and buried it inside the camp of Israel, but once the sin was recognized and the equivalent punishment meted out to him, (he was stoned and his body burnt to death in the Valley of Achor), and they heaped up a pile of rock upon him and named it: "the Valley of Achan." Then God told Joshua to "Take heart and try against **A'I.** once more" According to **Joshua 07:01-08, 26-29.**

So, just as how evil could not be tolerated in the promise land; evil cannot be tolerated in our lives today. We, like Israel must ruthlessly remove sin from our lives, before it takes total control of us. The Lord commanded Joshua to march around the City wall for seven straight days: According to **Chapter 06:03-04,** they were to go around it once for six days, (everyday) then on the seventh day they should compass the city seven times. It was not the expertise nor the type of ammunition of Israel that caused them to win the battle, but obedience to God's command: He told them to "take up the Ark of the Covenant, (which represents the presence of the Lord) and have seven priest carrying it and march at the front, blow the trumpet at your command, we are now fighting a conquered foe because the battle is already won, if we are fighting in the name of the Lord. The instructions given for that strange military maneuver was a test of Israel's obedience to God's instruction. Note carefully that the trumpets (or horns) that the priests blew were the ones that they blew in the religious festivals when they worshipped, so they could confidently used them in battle at the instruction of the Lord. According to: **Numbers 10: 01-09,** Thirty-nine years before the conquest of **A'I.** they were told: "When you go up to battle against the enemy who is oppressing you, sound a blast on the trumpet then you will be remembered by the Lord your God, and be rescued from your enemies: I am the Lord your God."

It seems clear to me here that the mouth that blesses the Lord continuously, and praises Him in sincerity is more authoritative to subdue the enemy in battle. It is for the same reason why, when the enemies ride in against us like a flood then the Holy Spirit lift up a standard against them. There is usually a manifestation of shouts against them, and usually they are scattered.

The children of Israel were a disobedient set of people, although they were God's chosen people. Over one million persons left Egypt for Canaan however, only Caleb and Joshua (of those who left Egypt) reached the promised land. The others who reached, were born in the wilderness.

I will mention five groups of persons as it relates to **Types** as follows:

1. **Romans 07:23** "Canaan is a **Type** of our higher Christian life to be won by warfare."
2. **Ephesians 06:12** "The Canaanites were a type of Spiritual enemies (the very reason why God drove them out of the land and gave it the Israelites."
3. **1st.Timothy 06:12** "The warfare of Israel is a Type of the fight of Faith"
4. **Hebrews 04:09** "Israel's rest is a Type of rest for the soul."
5. **Hebrews 12:01** "The Canaanite partly subdued is a Type of besetting sin."

Conclusion

Quote 1st. Kings 03:14 "And if thou will walk in my ways, to keep my statures and my commandments as your father David did walk, then I will lengthen thy days."

Quote Psalm 18:30 "As for God, His way is perfect; the word of the Lord is tried He is a buckler to all who trust Him

Living in obedience to God's words is not a task, rather it is a process; so, obedience should become a life-style, both for civil and divine authorities.

Chapter 26
Prayer The Foundation For Success

Scripture Readings: 1st Chronicles 04:09 – 10 (Jabez Prayer)

It was believed that Jabez became an ancestor of the kings' tribe of Judah although his parents are not mentioned in the chronicles. The NIV states that he was more honorable than all his brethren. His mother named him Jabez because he was born in pain, so later when Jabez found out why his mother named him so, he cried out to God for four things.

1. Bless me Indeed
2. Enlarge my territory
3. Let your hands be with me.
4. Keep me from harm so I will be free from pain

God granted him his requests and today Jabez is remembered for his prayer request more than for his heroic acts. It is important to note that we as sanctioned of rewarded for the things we do in life so, let us be very careful, because we are going to reap the rewards whatever we have sown.

It was at the point when Jabez discovered his aptitude that he developed the attitude to make that great difference in his own life, today that great move is a motivation for many. Sir Winston Churchill said "Attitude is a little thing that makes a big difference" and Dr. Myles Monroe said: Jabez did not just pray for physical protection from harm and pain because he lived in a world filled with evil, but he also asked God to protect him from the avoidable evils, and evil thoughts, that come our way from time to time, because desires and actions first begin within us before they are manifested outwardly; for the difference between the thought of evil and the evil thoughts is the encouragement it receives.

All persons, but especially those of us who are placed in leadership positions, should look closely at self first, before we even venture to take the next step. Let us first identify the place we are at, and the purpose God wants us to fulfill. It is at this point where we discover the true reasons for our existence, that a leader is born, and it is only when a true leader is born that one will lead with a much greater sense of significance, and it is only then that our purpose will become much clearer to others and to us..

Brothers and sisters, let us through the use of prayer and fasting, develop an attitude like Winston Churchill who said "It is the little things that make the difference with attitude" So let us start making new and different attitudes in order to get the different and the favorable results we would like to have.

Many of us want to be more than just an ordinary servant,

- We want to be the head and not the tail,
- We want, like Jabez that our prayers will be answered
- In order to achieve these we need to get rid of the evil thoughts within our hearts; less the good Lord will not hear us.

St. Matthew 06: 05-18 "Instructions concerning Prayer) it states clearly that the heart must be in proper condition in order that our prayers may be answered"

2nd. Chronicles 07: 14 (Gives us the conditions for successful Contrition)

In it, it is written: "If my people, who are called by my name, shall humble themselves and pray, and seek my face, and turn from their wicked ways, then will I hear from heaven, and will forgive their sins, and will heal their land."

Conclusion

Leaders and aspiring leaders ought to be yielding ourselves fully to the Master's call, if ye are going to be successful, because our natural abilities alone will not be sufficient to withstand the test of time. We need to depend on God minutely for His help and guidance. We will need to do the following things.

1. Morning devotions
2. Evening prayers
3. Solitary Communions
4. Prayers of confession
5. Public Prayers
6. All Night Prayer Meetings (Sometimes)

Prayer is the foundation to a successful ministry, and there is no ways around it.

God Bless, have a successful Ministry.

Chapter 27
Safety And Success Through Service

Reading: Psalm 112: 05 "A good man deals graciously and lends, He will guide his affairs with discretion"

Deuteronomy 16:16-17 states "We should give according to our ability. Giving is not just money or service, but also of our talent and our time" and Jacob said **in Genesis 28:22**. "Of all that Thou shall give me I will surely give the tenth unto Thee" (this is separate and apart from one's occupation). If we are called to serve, then the Jacob's experience that we model is separate from our occupation. So we should make time for service to God, to our community and our fellowmen. One doctor said recently on a radio program that: "To continue living on planet earth, then the rent we pay is our service to our fellowmen."

Paul said to the Philippians brethren as is recorded in **Philippians 02:04:** "Look not every man on his own things, but every man also on the things of others". So, he exhorted them to love, unity and service". At this unprecedented time in the world's history when the common term being used is: "The New Norm" here and now we are given an opportunity to perfect our service to God; which is in fact, our service to our fellowmen. So Jesus communicated to his disciples in **St. Matthew 25:31–46** when he gave the **Service Test,** then in **Verse 40** he said: "Verily I say unto you. Inasmuch as ye have done it unto one of the least of these my brethren, ye have done it unto me". This is to say when we love God, in essence we are saying that we love people, and to the contrary when we hate people then it is God that we hate as well.

Looking at the subject at hand, the time suggests that we make concerted efforts to be different by our approach to each other and to kingdom activities and expectations, because some of us, we are Christians alright, but we don't practice giving back at all, we are only concerned about getting, getting, getting. We don't give back to our parents, nor, our siblings, nor to our Church and community, all we are concerned about is, how will it benefit us? The point cannot be overstated, there are the fifteen established Spiritual Disciplines that are practiced by Pentecostals and even though it is looked at by some, with least importance, the facts remain, that service is the most important of them all. A friend of mine was on vacation in the United States of America once but things weren't going well with him then, in his moment of despair he got out of the house and went for a walk, as he past a church gate, he was prompted to go in and ask for prayer, for a change in his circumstances. So, he went to the Priest for blessings, he anticipated that he would be anointed with oil and be prayed for by the priest; but the priest told him: "Do a good deed to a less fortunate person everyday and your success will be guaranteed". That was similar to the rich ruler was told to sell all that he had and give to the poor. However from that day forward my friend took a new approach to life.

There are a few things that we can do differently.

1. Make people feel important.
2. Grow the service attitude to higher heights every day.
3. Make service a rule and always remember that, the support you give to others is the only hurdle between you and what you want to be
4. Serve, Serve, Serve. Even when a risk is involve sometimes.

Acts chapter **10:38-39** The Apostle Peter gave an account of how God anointed Jesus with the power of the Holy Ghost and Power, equipping Him for service; then he went forth doing good and healing those that were oppressed of the devil. Like Jesus, we must take pleasure in serving others, some people bask in the fact of being served by others but never want to be a servan. **Acts 20:35** states: "I have showed you all things, how that so laboring ye ought to support the weak, and to remember the words of the Lord Jesus, how it said. It is more blessed to give than to receive" So then the real blessing that is associated with service, is not to be at the receiving end. Clearly note here that service and serving are two tests that we continue to fail, because some of us always only want, want, want; rather than to give, give, give.

In the recent past I reiterated the point that sometimes there is a set of persons who, when a call is made for money even for a very good cause, they may not have the money to give to the call, so we could sometimes give service instead, toward the said call, however they don't even give service either, so they will always remain at the lower end of the socio-economic ladder. With the sowing and reaping model, what can we do differently, what will we do differently.

I will seek to benchmark Samuel in his youthful days, at a point when he did not yet know the lord. According to **1ˢᵗ Samuels 03:01-21.** Service is a good trait for youths to take on. Samuel became the last of the Judges in Israel and formed the transitional link between the Eras of the Judges and the Kings. He served Eli at a time when he was laid down and his eyes went dim. V.02. For him, who did not yet know the Lord, yet he demonstrated the right attitude of a servant; it played well in his favour and paid a high dividend. It was while he was serving Eli in the absence of his (Eli's) two sons: Hoph'ni and Phin'e-has whose reports were very bad. At the time when the Lord called Samuel he was so inexperienced he could not even recognized the voice, or the call of the God, neither did he know that God knew his name; moreso to have called him. But Eli guided him and aided him in answering the call.

Conclusion

From time to time we impress others by our expressions that are not truly in harmony with who we truly are. In that case we would have deceived ourselves and may be deceived others, but we should seek to be true representative of Christ, and that should rightfully be so by:

- Our actions
- Our speaking
- Our behavior
- And by our business principles

We should all pledge today to grow the service attitude first (which is giving, giving, giving.) and always remember that our success and safety depends on our service to our fellowmen; Brethren it is important that we learn to love people. Like Jesus does, which is done by practicing, practicing, practicing, until we learn how to be genuine.

God bless you all as we take on this one, "Safety and success through service" as one of the NEW NORMS.

Chapter 28
The Greatness Of Humility

Read Exodus 05:01-10 (Sp. V. 02)

Introduction

I will use the matter of Pharaoh's ignorance and pride as a preamble to the study at hand, the attitudes that led to his downfall and compare and contrast his era to our present generation to show that "people are the same everywhere whether they are white or black" as said by former U.S. President Bill Clinton.

What relevance has youths and young adult with the life of Daniel and why is the book of Daniel so difficult to understand, however I would want to benchmark Daniel's determination and use it to guide us during this time, because there is nothing new under the sun.

How old was Daniel then?

All people, 20 years **old,** or **older** were condemned to perish in the wilderness (except Caleb **and** Joshua). So, it **is** estimated that **Daniel** was about 17 years old when **he** went to **Babylon**, during the third year of Jehoiakim, king of Judah. **That** means **Daniel** was 36 years **old** when Jerusalem **and** Solomon's temple were destroyed. *(36-17=19 years later)*

This passage of scripture speaks of: "Pharaoh's ignorance and pride"

I will attempt to address two key words from the Text: Greatness & Humility.

Greatness is defined by the Oxford Dictionary as follows: enormity, vastness, not being simple, the magnitude or importance of something.

Humility: Humbleness, meekness, modesty or being unassuming in nature.

(**My thought**: "Humility does not mean softness; one can be very humble, yet very firm")

I will attempt to benchmark **DANIEL** as the perfect example of humility.

The Book of Daniel is one of the most complex books of the Bible. It's Author is believed to be Ezekiel and it is a companion to the Book of Revelation in its imagery which is very mysterious. An attempt to properly define its contents; concerning the facts of the events of human history has produced an endless conflict of opinions among candid scholars but there are two things they always agreed on, they are:

1. That the prophesies represent a partly veiled revelation of future events in secular and sacred history.
2. That the visions point to the ultimate triumph of God's kingdom over all satanic and world powers.

Daniel was a contemporary of Shadrach, Meshach, Abednego, Nebuchadenezzar, Belshazzar & Darius. (There are questions as to whether Daniel was the same person as Belteshazzar, **There were Belshazzar & Belteshazzar,)** according to **Daniel 01:6-7 & 04:19**

While the prophet Ezekiel was ministering to the Babylonian Captives of which Daniel and his three friends Shadrach, Meshach & Abednego were among thousands of his countrymen who were taken captives, when Jerusalem was siege and defeated by Nebuchadenezzar the Babylonian King. The men were screened, and the brightest, sharpest, fittest and those without physical defects, were selected to study the Babylonian's language and literature over a three years period **Vs. 05 & 06** and be qualified to serve in some key positions in the Babylonian's Kingdom.

In line with the assignments given to those four special Youths they were given new names and titles reflecting their responsibilities as follows:

The Name Daniel means: "GOD IS MY JUDGE" his characteristics are:

- **Self control: Chapter 01:08 &10:03**
- **Courage: Chapter 05:22, 23**
- **Integrity: Chapter 06:04**
- **Prayerfulness: Chapter 02:17**
- **Humility: Chapter 10:17**
- **Spiritual Vision: Chapter 07: 09-12, 10;5,6**

Daniel's was changed to: Belteshazzar   meaning: Protect the life of the King.

Hananiah's was changed to: **Shadrach** meaning Command of Aku; (a Sumerian God)

Michael's was changed to: **Meshach** meaning who is what Auk is?

Azariah's was changed to: **Abednega** meaning servant of Nebo.

So, Daniel became King Darius's most trusted advisor and he was the third highest ruler in the kingdom **(2)** the same night king Bel-shazzer was slain **(3)** at that point he was 62 years old, when Darius the Median took the kingdom.

Daniel and his friends were taken captive and were deported to Babylon by Nebuchadenezzar the Babylonian king. They demonstrated the ability to do well of such they were taken from their homes in Judah   and was exiled in Babylon. In **605 B.C.** Although they were young they did not make their youthfulness prevail in youthful mistakes, rather they exhibited outstanding traits, and as a result they were chosen to work in the King's Palace.

He (**Daniel**) was gifted with the ability to interpret dreams, explain riddles and solve difficult problems. He was humble, very prayerful, careful about what he ate, from whom he ate, and most of all, he was true to his faith. According to Daniel **Chapter 05,** one of Daniel's prophetic utterances was fulfilled on the very night when they saw the hand writing on the wall. That the Babylonian kingdom would be divided, and be given to the Medes and the Persian. So Daniel became one of Darius most trusted advisor, so much so that his privileged position, angered other administrators to the point that they plotted his death by telling the King of his constant prayer to his sovereign Lord. That was however another occasion for him to prove God's goodness towards his servants.

Daniel was determined, and his determination caused him to be thrown in the den of hungry lions, (not just a lion's den, because a lion's den could at some point be empty because he decided that he would not defile himself with the King's meat, nor his wine nor worship the golden image) So God locked the jaws of the lions for Daniel's sake, because He is our defense and our very present help in trouble.

According to **Daniel 04:28-32; In 570 B. C.**"Neb-u-chad-nez'ar the king of Babylon boasted of the great Babylon that he built for the house of his kingdom, by his own might and power and to honor his majesty"

In **Daniel 5:23-26** it is stated that by **538 B.C.** which is 32 years later Neb-u-chad-nez'ar's grandson Bel-shazzer became the reigning king of Babylon, so he took the vessels of the temple and used them in the great feast he planned and conducted, It was then that he saw the Hand of God writing on the wall.

(Me'ne): God has numbered thy kingdom and finished it.

(Te'kel): Thou are weighted in the balance and found wanting (According to the message: "you   certainly do not weigh much")

(Pe-res): Thy kingdom is divided and is given to the Medes and the Persians. **Nb.** Here the Medes and the Persians had the world powers then.

Verses 29-31 speak of (1) how Daniel was promoted ruler in the kingdom he was to be third highest in the kingdom.

The book of Daniel though narrative in its scope, demonstrates clearly that although Daniel was so well accomplished and at such outstanding heights of the great men, (both reached and kept,) he for sure remained **HUMBLE** and **STEADFAST** in his faith. Although the book is largely narrative in its scope, concerning Biography and History, there is no other book in the Old Testament that contains such thrilling events and divine Interpositions and victories over moral conflicts like it.

The true interpretation of the details of the visions is not clear

There are six main conflicts to which to which His loyalty to God wins.

1. Between pagans, self-indulgence and conscientious abstinence in promoting health. **Chapter 01 08-15.** Abstinence wins.
2. Between Pagan Magic and heavenly wisdom, concerning the interpretation of dreams. **Chapter 02 01-47. Divine wisdom wins.**

3. Heathen idolatry arrayed against loyalty to God. **Chapter 03:01-30.** Loyalty to God wins.

4. A pagan king's pride arrayed against Divine Sovereignty, He turned out to eat grass like the beast of the field. **Chapter 04:04-37.** God wins.

5. **Impious Sacrilege arranged against reverence for sacred objects (with the hand writing on the wall Belshazzar dethroned). Chapter 05: 01 – 30. Reverence wins.**

6. Malicious plotting between the providence of God over His saints (The lions mouth stopped. **Chapter 06 01 – 28. Providence wins.**

It is to be noted that the Book of Daniel is one of the most difficult books of the Bible because it contains prophesies that are not easily understood.

Daniel Chapter 07	Many commentators see the **Four beasts** as representing the **Great Empires: (1) Babylon (2) Medo-Persia (3) Greece & (4) Rome.** Followed by a vision of the **Coming Messiah**
Daniel Chapter 08	Another period of **Medo-Oersian and Grecian h**istory appears under the figure of the beast.
Daniel Chapter 09	Contains Daniel's prayer and a veiled prophecy of the time of the coming of the Messiah.
Daniel Chapter 10-12	Contains additional far-reaching predictions and revelations of future events. These three chapters have been the battle ground of theological controversy with many varied interpretations

St. Luke 22: 26 states who would be the greatest in the Spiritual Kingdom **(Do a demonstration using a belt with a buckle)** that there is really no comparison with God, because He is Immeasurable, but in order to get this point across, when God is compared with man I will attempt to use a belt to assist in bringing out the point.

When folded into two equal parts, you may have humility in moderation, yet the part with the buckle represents God, while the other end represents man, note here that the end with the buckle will surely weigh more than the other end.

So shorten the end without buckle which part represents man, and the part with the buckle represents God. Then it will definitely be more in length and weight, the other part which represents man, will naturally become **little,** and the part representing God will becomes **more** when compared;

So adjust it a second time in the same direction, so that man becomes **less**, and God become most, then the third time making it all with the Buckle at the top, then, it will be all of God and **none** of man.

So the greatness of humility is, when we give ourselves to God that is humility indeed. because man now becomes nothing. It is at that point that God will certainly use us to a greater extent, and in whatever way He pleases. (When we give ourselves away.) (Song: I give myself away)

Conclusion

My Youths it is in difficult and stressful time like these that the metal of our make-up is tested. **Eg. Whether or not we maintain our faithfulness during a time when we are most times out of the presence of our brethren and are not congregating physically as per usual. But in trueness is, what do we do?**

1. **How do we behave when no one is watching?**
2. **Do we read our bibles? do we pray enough?**

3. **Do we still pay our tithes, and give our offering?**
4. **Do we care about the less-fortunate and the elderly?**
5. **Do we stand up well?**

Humility says: "Be kind, work hard, stay humble, smile often, stay loyal, keep being honest, travel when possible, never stop learning, be thankful, and amazing things will happen for you." **(By: Conan Obrien)**

So: Be strong, not weak, be kind, not rude, be proud, not arrogant, be humble, but not timid, like Daniel, So great, yet so humble.

Chapter 29
Abiding In The Shepherd's Care

The well known scripture that points to the Shepherd's Care is Psalm 23 otherwise known as the: "Shepherds Psalm" the other scriptures in the chain point to the many features of the sheep. So, they speak to the shepherd, the sheep, and the sheepfold, the sheepshearer, the sheep market, the Shepherd, the shepherd's bag, the shepherd's rod and staff. The better thing about the subject is, it is not just an Old Testament account, but is equally represented in the New Testament.

It is believed that the sheep was one of the earliest animals of the wild to be domesticated, (maybe over 3000 B.C) they were also the most used animal for religious sacrifice. It is believed that the tenderness of its meat could be a factor, besides its wool was used for clothing, their tails contains a large amount of fat, their horns were used to store oil, and also to trumpet the call to Israel for their religious rites, they were used for milk even more than for meat. The sheep served so many purposes; (no wonder Jesus is called the Lamb of God)

The Sheepfold: St John 10:01 Regard it as a place of protection, where the sheep would be kept from wandering, or from getting lost, they were not usually covered, but their walls were covered with thorns to keep robbers out.

The Sheep Market: According to **St. John 05:02** there was a sheep market in Jerusalem beside the pool of Be-thes'da, the pool which had five porches, and it was the favorite spot for impotent folks to hang-out and wait for their healing. The purpose of the market was for the farmers to trade their sheep.

The Sheep Sheerer: Was a person whose duty was to shear the sheep at the designated times and season, to produce wool for warm clothing. He was not necessarily the owner of the flock, nor the shepherd, his occupation was a seasonal work, he knows how to sheer and when to so that the sheep maintains good health. According to **Genesis 38: 12:13**

The Shepherd was also known as the Sheep Master he usually carries a bag, a rod and a staff.

The Shepherd's Bag: Was his primary container, he would carry his snacks or any other small items in it, in the event of David and Goliath (the Philistine giant whom he slew) in order to remove the reproach from Israel. His bag was the container of the five stones he took from the brook, He only needed to use one to accomplish his task, and maintained the possibilities of taking on any other of Goliath's team member, had they foolishly approached him, bearing in mind that the man who carried Goliath's shield was not far off. So we need to always understand that there is hardly a lonely enemy, usually there are associates **1st. Samuels 17: 40-57**

The Shepherd's Rod: Is a symbol of authority, the Psalmist David said in chapter **23:04;** It gives comfort even at the point of death, and in life it guides and corrects.

The Shepherd's Staff According to **Psalm 23:04:** Is a source of comfort (The crook on your staff comforts me, even at the point of death, it carries a divine presence, it gives divine protection and divine confidence.

Christ The Shepherd: (Eight key features of Shepherding)

1. He is a Spiritual watchman,
2. He is the divine teacher.

3. He is tender and always seeks for the lost sheep.
4. The shepherd as the Provider, He feeds His sheep.
5. The Sacrificial Shepherd, that gives His life for His sheep.
6. He being the provider according to **Psalm 23:05** The NIV puts it this way: "He feeds his flock with a six course meal, a six course meal is not an ordinary meal, it is one that is usually partake of in a very special setting, and most times by the elites. However when God blesses you and provides for you, It is marvelous in the eyes of others.

A meal served in courses makes any occasion feel special. The usual evening meal may be served in three courses that consist of salad, an entree or main plate and dessert. A meal expanded to six courses means adding an appetizer, soup and palate cleanser prior to the main course, and serving the salad after. The order is usually appetizers, soup, palate cleanser, entree, salad and dessert. Setting the table for multiple courses requires more pieces of dinner ware, glass ware and flatware. And requires more planning, to get it right is usually not so simple.

So when you are blessed and highly favoured to be eating a six course meal repeatedly and not as a one-off occasion, those who are able to do that are dub to be highly flavored, highly decorated, and is usually happy, to be getting special treatment. That is a part of the blessing plan for His people and the greatest of all He does it in the presence of our enemies.

When David wrote in **Psalm 23:05** it was after he made great achievements, won many battles, removed national reproach, tore lions with his bare hands, he did all in an effort to protect the sheep, he had been through a lot before he was given the table in the presence of his enemies, In the ancient Near Eastern culture, it was customary to anoint a person with fragrant oil as lotion, this gesture was usually performed at a banquet, the host were expected to protect their guests at all costs. God offers the protection of a host even when enemies surround us. So when our ways please God He will protect us like He protected David.

The secular settings are used to relate the blessings that the Good Shepherd has in store for us His flock, and all we need to do is to be faithful to Him and He will give us the desires of our hearts. **Jeremiah 03:15** States: "And I will give you Pastors accordingly, which shall feed you with knowledge and understanding" and **Jeremiah 23:04:** "And I will set up shepherds over them which shall feed them, and they shall fear no more, nor be dismayed' neither shall they be lacking, saith the Lord."

1. The Shepherd's love for the lost sheep. He said in **Jeremiah 50:06** "My people hath been lost sheep their shepherds have caused them to go astray, they have turned them away on the mountains, they have gone from mountains to hill, they have forgotten their resting place" and in **St. Matthew 15:24** Jesus answered and said: "I am not sent but the lost sheep of the house of Israel"

2. **The Risen Lamp: Hebrews 13: 02** States that Jesus the great Shepherd of the Sheep, through the blood of the everlasting covenant, brought Jesus from the dead, and **1ˢᵗ. Peter 05:04** speaks of Him crowning the faithful: "And when the Chief Shepherd shall appear, ye shall receive a crown that fadeth not away"

Conclusion

Christ the Shepherd, Christ the door to the fold: Clearly stated in **St. John 10:07-09:** "Jesus said unto them again, verily, verily, I say unto you. I am the door of the sheep, all that ever came before me are thieves and robbers, but the sheep did not hear them. I am the door by me if any man enters in, he shall be saved and shall go in and out and find pasture." According to the MacArthur's Student Bible; It is the shepherd that leads the sheep out of the pen, here he is the entrance to the pen that leads to the pasture, this echoes Jesus' words in chapter 14:06 where He exclaims that He is the only way to the father, This is the only way of salvation, as some Near Eastern shepherds slept in the gateway in order to guard their sheep. Jesus here describes Himself as the door. So neither can the sheep exit the fold, nor the wolves enter the fold without encountering the shepherd because the pastures in the Near Eastern land had no physical doors, only a single doorway, and usually the shepherd stretched himself across the door way with his back against the door-post, and in a sitting position with his legs across the way, it was so designed to make it compulsory that the doorway be managed by someone, who happened to be the shepherd; So in this regard. Jesus is our shepherd, with Him being the door we are protected from all harms, and I am convince, there can be no better way.

Chapter 30
Trust In The Lord And Make Him Our Refuge

Scripture Reading: Psalm 46: 1-11

V.01 "God is our refuge and strength, a very present help in trouble"

V.11 "The Lord of host is with us; the God of Jacob is our refuge"

Trust: "Firm belief in a person or thing, reliability, or strength, confident, expectation"

Refuge: Shelter from pursuits or danger, or trouble (a city of refuge for those guilty of manslaughter in ancient Israel, a house or institution for the homeless persons, to give shelter or, is resorted to in difficulties or distress) then the persons that seek such help; whether Religious or Political War, are called **Refugee.**

Jerusalem is a city located in the Middle East on a plateau in the Judean Mountains between the Mediterranean and the Dead sea. It is one of the oldest cities in the world, and has no river of its own yet. The Musician said to the sons of Ko'rah in **Psalm 46:04.** (With reference to Jerusalem) "There is a river, the streams whereof shall make glad the city of God, the holy place of the tabernacles of the most High".

Many great cities have rivers flowing through them, sustaining the people's lives, by making agriculture possible and facilitating trade with other cities; Although Jerusalem has no river, they had God, who, like a river sustains His people's lives, as long as God lives among His people that city is invincible, unbeatable, and unshakable.

The world is going through embarrassing, troubling and distressful times presently, and our country is no exception. The church is even assaulted in very serious ways; the reverence, respect and mercy it once enjoyed seems to have expired, but God sits high and looks low and we only need Him to cover and shelter us from all doom and destruction, and shelter us like how the hens shelter their chickens. The NIV puts it this way: God is always there to help, providing refuge, security and peace; His power is complete, and his ultimate victory is certain, and He will not fail to rescue us from harm. **(In scripture, rivers are symbols of divine blessings.)**

The security of the saints is different; it was guaranteed from the very foundation of the world. In **Psalm 91:01-02** David outlined it as follows "He that dwelleth in the secret place of the most High shall abide under the shadow of the Almighty. I will say of the Lord, He is my refuge and my fortress: My God, in Him will I trust" **Proverbs 03:24** states: "When thou liest down, thou shalt not be afraid yea, thou shalt lie down, and Thy sleep shall be sweet".

There are only two New Testament accounts that I have found regarding the word refuge (directly) they were given by Paul and Peter. For Paul it was to the **Hebrews** in chapter **13:06** "So that we may boldly say The Lord is my helper, and I will not fear what man shall do unto you" and **Hebrews 06:18** "That by two immutable things in which it is impossible for God to lie, we might have a strong consolation, who have fled for **refuge** to lay hold upon the hope set before." And **1ˢᵗ Peter 03:13** "And who is it that will harm you, if ye be followers of that which is good"

It is clear in my mind that there is a line of demarcation drawn between the Christians and the Non-Christians where safety is concerned. Let's look at **Proverbs 03: 21-35** and Verses **32 & 33** and I quote: "For the froward is an abomination to the Lord, but His secret is with the righteous. The curse of the Lord is in the house of the wicked, but He bless the habitation of the just" and **Proverbs 12:21** *s*aid "There shall no evil happen to the just; but the wicked shall be filled with mischief" (evil) The Major Prophet **Isaiah** in **32:18** reads: "And my people shall dwell in a peaceable habitation, and in sure dwellings, and in quiet resting places" while **Jeremiah 23:06** (Which is a Messianic Safety Prophecy) states that: "In the days Judah shall be saved, and Israel shall dwell safely; and this is the name whereby He shall be called" **The Lord our righteousness.**

The Song (I quote) "The Lord our Rock in Him we hide, a shelter in a time of storm, secure what-ever I'll be tide, A shelter in the time of storm . Oh Jesus is rock in a weary land, a shelter in the time of storm".

So; this I say let us make the Lord our trust, and our **REFUGE!**

Chapter 31
Effectual Fervent Prayer, And Hindrances To Prayer

Read: Genesis 04: 25-26, St. John 17:20

From as early as the first generation as is recorded in Geneses 04: 26 (AKA) in the beginning of time, first family Adam, Eve, and their son Seth, who became the father of Enosh, they began to call upon the name of the Lord. So in the process of time prayer became universal. Then in 1023 B.C. David spoke of the need for public prayers, Then Jesus did His prayer publicly after his baptismal Service. St. Luke 03:21-22.

So, many methods, and varied styles, and posture in which it is done, and can be done, both before Christ came in the flesh, and after. Examples: through the following methods and styles.

- Kneeling - Ephesians 03:14
- Standing - St. Mark 11:25
- In Secret - St. Matthew 06:06
- Private Prayers - St. Mark 01: 35
- Public Prayer - St. Luke 03:21
- All-night Prayer - St. Luke 06:12
- Universal Prayers - Psalm 65:02
- Prayer for Food - St. Matthew 06 :11
- Prayer for the Church - St. John 17:20
- Unwise Prayers - St. Matthew 20: 20-22

So, no matter what type or style of prayer we do, it is the state of the heart that matters most; "Confess you fault one to another, and pray one for another, that ye may be healed. The **Effectual Fervent** prayers of the Righteous man that availeth much" **James 05:16**

Effectual: "Answering its purpose, sufficient to produce"

Fervent: Hot, glowing, intense, ardent.

St. John 09:31 "Now I know that God heareth not Sinners, but if any man be a worshipper of God, and doeth His will, him He heareth" The interpretation of this scripture has been controversial among many scholars for centuries, however, David said in **Psalm 66:16-20** "If I regard iniquity in my heart, the Lord will not hear me" The NIV puts it this way, and I quote: "Come and listen, all you who fear the God; let me tell you what he has done for me, I cried out to Him with my mouth, His praise was on my tongue. **V18 "If I cherished sin in my heart, the Lord would not have listened, But God has surely listened, and heard my voice in prayer. Praise God, who has not rejected my prayer or withheld His love from me".**

The disciples asked Jesus, because they were convinced that there must be a right way to pray, rather than; to each his own. In St. Luke 11 Jesus told them as follows, as a procedure:

You must first worship Me

Then ask for bread

Then for forgiveness, which is hinged on our willingness to forgive others

After which we should ask for a way to escape temptation. And continue to be hospitable to others. Other than that our Prayers would be hindered.

In the understanding and the application of the statement. Then clearly we are all sinners, but if we go to God with worshipful attitude then He hears our prayers.

Below are nine things that can hinder our Prayers:

1. **Secrets Sins - Psalms 66:18**
2. **Indifference - Proverbs 01:28**
3. **Neglect of Mercy - Proverbs 21:13**
4. **Despising the Law - Proverbs 28:09**
5. **Blood Guiltiness - Isaiah 01:15**
6. **Iniquity - Isaiah 59:02 & Micah 03:04**
7. **Stubbornness - Zechariah 07:13**
8. **Instability - James 01:06-07**
9. **Self Indulgence - James 04:03**

Read Romans 08:26:28 - (The intercession of the Holy Spirit)

Prayer is one of **13** Spiritual Disciplines, These **Disciplines will only Make Our Faith Stronger.**

It is believed that these **13** primary spiritual activities were practiced by Jesus and prescribed for all believers: they are: "study, **prayer**, fasting, confession, worship, fellowship, rest, celebration, service, generosity, journaling, chastity and disciple-making." here is a model prayer: It was sent to me by a friend.

Dear God.

"I kneel down before you at this moment

Please enlighten whatever is dark in me

Strengthen whatever is weak in me

Mend whatever is broken in me

Heal whatever is sick in me

And revive whatever peace and life has died in me.

This is my prayer for me, my family, my friends, my enemies

And even those who hate me. Amen."

Sometimes we can't even pray perfectly, because the truth and honesty with which we ought to pray, is clouded by our situations, circumstances sometimes cast a shadow over our consciences, as a result the main points on which we should focus are left out of our prayer, but the lesson in: **Romans 08:26:** "Likewise the spirit also helped our infirmities, for we know not what we should pray for as we ought, but the spirit itself makes intersession for us with groaning which cannot be uttered."

Read#1602 KJV page 1434 (HS. dwelling in the believers) the disciples had questions for Jesus at a time when it seemed there were uncertainties regarding prayers. So in St. Luke 11:01-04

He taught them how to pray, it is known today as the model prayer. And it is practiced by some people as a routine prayer. Others used as a defense against evil spirit. Once they feel a sense of insecurity, then one can be assured that there is ground to repeat that prayer; after which they would then be at peace with others and themselves. But defense is definitely not the only aspect of the prayer. So it must be done with utmost diligence.

Chapter 32
Preach It, demonstrate It, And If Necessary, Use Words

The **St. Luke 05:01-11** account, is one that had to do with when Christ preached from Peter's ship, it goes on to say: as the people pressed upon Him to hear the word of God, He stood by the Lake of Gen-nets'-ret (otherwise call the Sea of Galilee) from where he saw two empty ships and He entered into one which was owned by Peter, at a point when the men were   washing their nets which was a practice by the fishermen of the day. Whether or not they caught fish they were supposed to wash their nets after each fishing trip to get rid of sea weeds and be made clean and ready for the next fishing trip.

To **Preach** is to: sermonize it, speak it, or to lecture it.

To **Demonstrate:** is to lay it bare, make obvious express it and show it.

Preachers need not be hypocrites by not living what they preach, or by not preaching what they live. Our actions speak much louder than our words, so, when people see what we do, it resonates with them much longer than only the spoken words. One of the reformers (it is believed to be John Knox in 1831) said: "Let the ministers preach it, and if necessary use words". He further said the words must be preached by saved men, called men, men who are sent, and as we advanced the journey, we remain saved.

Luke, the physician, expounded the story of the miraculous catch of fishes in a similar way as Matthew and Mark did, but in my opinion with a little more detail than the other two, perhaps, because of his academic ability, while Mark and Luke were not included in the inner circle of the twelve disciples like Matthew and John. Mark however was said to have accompanied Paul on his first missionary journey (Acts 13:13) while Luke was a physician.

This account happened around A.D. 55 to AD 65, note though that John had not written his book until A.D. 85. It is interesting to note that although Jesus was born in Bethlehem on a farm and had no fishing experience, because, according to the history, Jesus was a carpenter after the likes of his father Joseph yet he marveled them with his knowledge of the trade,   and the level of productivity that was gained. Interestingly he called some men who had no formal theological training save and except from what he taught them while they were on the Job, and they learnt through obedience to His word.

Today, all of us who did not meet Peter personally, now do through religious history. The record of his experience with the miraculous draught of fishes is a clear demonstration of the   supernatural power that Jesus possesses.

It is marvelous to note that God is no respecter of persons. This is evident where Jesus just went into Peter's boat without seeking his permission, not even his consent, just like that, after he went in, he called Peter in, gave him a briefing, then He sent him out to fish. So as soon as he returned from his fishing trip, Jesus changed his occupation. St. Luke 05: 10: "Fear not; from henceforth you shall catch men" V11. I Quote "And when they had brought their ships to land, they forsook all and followed them."

In order to advance the kingdom of God, obedience is one of the most important requirements, when Peter returned from his fishing trip, and just realizing a new and different way to catch fish, which included a far greater level of productivity having not topped the level of catch, in any single fishing trip, nor had any of his colleges done that before. (His net broke) and he had to beckon to his partner, to: "come and help". Here we see that success comes through obedience. So Paul suddenly changed his life around, by making a spontaneous shift of his career from being a **Fisherman** to become **"Fishers-of-men."** (A sacrifice is the giving up something, for something else of a greater value) So Peter changed his profession and years of experience to a brand new one with rather strange responses, fishes don't oppose view like people but are rather subjective, now Peter had to learn new arts and cultures,

Some of us want to be successful, but not at the expense of being obedient. We love to, and or, want to do as we like, and think that nobody in authority should talk to us about policies and procedures. It is clear here that after Jesus taught Peter how to catch fish, how to break nets, how to signal to his partners to come and help him, (team work) then the non experienced, nontraditional fisherman taught the all time traditional recurring generational inherited family trait, to the regional fisherman how to catch fish on familiar turf, and then He said to him, "You shall no more catch fish, but you shall from now on catch men."

Conclusion

When Jesus calls a man and rearranges his life, there is no logical stopping, no amount of badmouthing, or sabotaging, or ganging, nor scheming can stop him. People have to get out of your way because when you launch out in the deep, especially at a time when not even you expect it and your net breaks then some traditional fisherman will have to wonder what's going on. Only then will some people know that it is neither your will nor ways, but it is the Lord's, for He has the final say, when the kingdom of God is advanced and we, by our demonstration of His power, have helped to advance it then God takes

HIs praise, gets his glory and the blessings will be evident in the drawing of men unto Himself

Chapter 33
Remain Faithful (Even) In Your Trials

Reading: Deuteronomy 07:09

"Know therefore that the Lord thy God, He is God, the faithful God, which keeps His covenant and mercy toward them that love Him, and keep His commandments to a thousand generations. If the prophecy of Moses is accurate, or even if it is only figurative, then I am glad that I am included; so, for sure, I am a part of that promise. That is why you can't stop me from loving my Lord; or from boasting in this common salvation, because I am a promise and I am a possibility. Whether my possibility is with a Capital "P" or even with a common "P" when Christ is in your life, it is alright, because little is much when God is in it. I am sure that He is in my life!

And the new world is only 6,020 years old, So, when factored by the 30 years generation principle, then 1,000 generations, when multiplied by 30 years then it gives approximately 30,000 years, which is equivalent to 201 generations so God's mercies is still available, and more-so still plenteous towards them that fear Him and keep His covenant of love.

From Creation to the flood is:	2,000 years	
From the flood to the birth of Christ is:	2,000 years	=4.000 years
From the birth of Christ to the end of the twentieth century is:	2,000 years	=6,000 years
And from the end of the twentieth century to date is:	0,020 years	=6,020 years

No wonder the Song writer: William R. Newell wrote in **1868** which song was revised it in **1956,** and Daniel B. Towner also wrote it in **1919. As follows:**

> *"Oh, the Love that drew salvation plan."*
>
> *Oh the grace that brought it down to man!*
>
> *Oh, the mighty gulf that God did span at Calvary."*
>
> ***Chorus***
>
> *Mercy there was great and grace was free.*
>
> *Pardon there was multiplied to me.*
>
> *There my burdened soul found liberty, at Calvary.*

That Salvation plan, though criticized by many, but it cannot be put down by any, because it was divinely designed by God Himself. The processed was executed by Jesus Christ, and sanctioned by the Holy Spirit, accepted by the apostles taught by the reformers, and is being carried out by you and me, and will be continued by our off-springs and will stand up firmly until Christ returns.

Faithfulness: Is defined by using other synonyms, like: Closeness, accuracy, truthfulness and authenticity. These traits are, and should be practiced by married people, but more-so by all Christians. Faithfulness is not, nor only related to marriage, but also to the church with which we are joined by a covenant, and to the Kingdom that is, the righteous System that governs our Relationship with God and our fellowmen.

Trial: "A trial, is a test, an examination, a check, a tryout, or an assessment" some people don't like Exams; they will tell you they have a phobia (A dread or fear for Exams.) even when they are the brightest in their class; but for the Christians our faithfulness is determined by our behavior during our trials.

It is said each trial only comes to make us stronger.

Proverbs 28:20 States that: A faithful man shall abound with blessings, but he that maketh haste to be rich shall not be innocent. V22. He that hasteth to be rich hath an evil eye, and considereth not that poverty shall come upon him.

Psalm 101: 06 David made a vow and a profession of Godliness when he wrote: Mine eyes shall be upon the faithful of the land, that they may dwell with me, he that walketh in a perfect way, he shall serve me.

V07. "He that worketh deceit shall not dwell with in my house, he that telleth lies shall not tarry in my sight"

V08. I will early destroy all the wicked of the land, that I may cut off all the wicked of the land, that I may cut off all the wicked doers, from the city of the Lord.

Conclusion

David said in his prayer. I want to walk a blameless path (not necessarily that you will be all together blameless) but to live in integrity, which is both a human effort and divine help from God. So, let us seek His help continuously, and remain faithful in our trials, and the God of love will certainly help us to be faithful to the end of our Christian journey, and note, It is not by might, nor by power, nor by human efforts only, but through and with the help of God!

The Song Says: "I must have the Savior with me, for I dare not walk alone. I must feel His presence near me, and His arms around me thrown, then my soul shall fear no ill, let Him lead me where He will. I will go without a murmur, and His footsteps follow still"

God Bless!

Chapter 34
Chosen Vessels

In **St. Matthew 22: 09-14** Jesus spoke to the people by a parable concerning the similarities of the Kingdom of Heaven and a certain king, whose son was getting married, and invitations were given to some special guests, who at the point of the wedding when, those that were given individual invitations, did not turn up, for some unknown reason. So the king was very disappointed because his special guests dishonored him, obviously he was insulted, he then responded to the insults of his Guests, by giving instructions again to his servants, to bid them to come, in light of the elaborate preparation that was made for them. **V.04** speaks of his dinner which was made of Oxen and other fatling, yet they still did not come; rather some went to their field, others to their merchandize, beside, they were so wroth that they went beyond just the ordinary insults, but to the extreme, they slew the king's servants, when the king heard of it, he was more angered; so, he sent out his army this time, with specific instructions to destroy them and burn up their cities.

Then the king sent another set of servants with new and different instructions this time. They were to go to the byways and they were to bid "whosesoever will" to come to his son's wedding, this time the wedding was furnished with guests (both good and bad) because his first choice was not realized, and the preparation was already made.

There are obviously different types of calls, example: Universal Calls, individual calls, calls to certain tribes, calls to certain race, and calls to certain cities. **St. Matthew 22:14** states that many are called but few are chosen. The word "chosen" appears **119** times in the English Bible;

91 times in the Old Testament, and **28** times in the New Testament; and states clearly that God did not choose people who were considered to be good, by human standards, but by God's. We also know according to **Jeremiah 10:23:** "O lord, I know that the way of man in not in himself; it is not in man that walketh to direct his steps". Therefore the only way one can be good is when their steps are ordered by God.

1st. Corinthians 01:27-31 puts it this way: "In God's Tool Chest. There are people of different orientation: strong and weak, rich and poor, wise and foolish, but He will used whomever He chooses, example: He has chosen the foolish things of the world to confound the wise and the weak things of the world, to confound the things which are mighty, and the base things of the world, and things that are despised, has God chosen. So that no man should glory in His presence, because He will not share His glory with anyone.

A very clear and forthright experience is how Jessie's eight sons profiled before Samuel, as is recorded in **1st. Samuels 16:01-14** Here we see that we may choose persons for specific positions based on our personal outlook, and assessment of them, or by the type and the quality of the lenses we are looking through, which may be far from Gods assessment of them, because man looks on the outward, but God looks on the heart. On the occasion of Samuel and Jesse's other sons, pertaining to the kingship of Israel. According to **Verses 6 & 7** When Samuel looked at E-li'ab with his fair countenance, his height and his stature, he said: "Surely the Lord's anointed is before us" but the Lord said: "no" then the other six brothers were called and were profiled as well; but the Lord refused them all; then it was not until the unsuspecting son: "David" who was the youngest of the eight sons, obviously he was left outside of the preferred loop, he was in the field at that time when the others were called and profiled as well, but the Lord refused them all. On the instruction of Samuel, they sent for

David. When he came, the Spirit of the Lord was upon Him and as he profiled, the Lord said to Samuel: "Arise and anoint him" So Samuel anointed him, in the presence of his brethren.

From time to time some of God's chosen persons are overlooked by those in authority; It may not be done deliberately sometimes, but through the errors of our humanness, and by the same process God's chosen persons are being kept out of their rightful place. However whenever this happens then, the Lord shows up because it is not about us, it is about Him, His chosen people and His plan for them. His blessings for His chosen can only be delayed, but it cannot be denied. Let us wait on the Lord and be of good courage, for He shall strengthen our hearts, (if only we will wait) wait I say on the Lord. **Psalm 27:14.**

Usually when an individual or a tribe is chosen they are protected by God, because He promised to protect His own, it will be brought to bear that there are uniqueness about the chosen, in the event of David; he was brave, skillful with music and skillful in battle, also he was a man after God's own heart.

There are different types of vessels made from different types of materials, example of: Ivory, gold, silver, bronze, brass, and earth, some to be used for the Lord's house and others for Baal worship. With the word vessel mentioned 171 times in the English Bible, and were designed for specific purposes. **2nd. Timothy 02: 20-21** States that in a great house, there are not only vessels of gold and of silver, but vessels of wood and of earth, and some to honor and some to dishonor, if a man therefore purge himself from these, he shall be a vessel unto honor, sanctified and meet for the masters use, and prepared unto every good works.

It is quite clear that some vessel are more costly than others, some maybe more frequently used than others, some may be more preferred than others; but they were all made to compliment each others, by being designed to be used for specific purposes. however with us as human beings; being referred to a vessels, it is for us to purge ourselves to be fit for the master's use, bearing in mind as the Apostle Paul said to the **Romans** in chapter **09:21:** "Hath not the potter power over the clay, of the same lump to make one vessel unto honor and another unto dishonor? And he also said to the **Thessalonians in Chapter 04:04:** "That every one of you should know how to posses your vessel in sanctification and honor" It is clear here that we are to make every effort to please God in all areas of our lives, so that we will be chosen vessels in the Lord's house.

Conclusion

So if you are liken unto the broken vessel, that was marred in the Potter's hand, then right now as you are reading this discourse, the Potter can do the make-over; if only you will let Him, be assured that He will make you into new vessels and will revived your souls again. As for me, Lord. I want to be more than an ordinary servant, and I want to be used as a vessel unto honour, because I believe that I am chosen.

How about you?

Chapter 35
Demonstrating Your Faith

Scripture Readings Hebrews 11: 01-06

Demonstrate: To demonstrate is to reveal, exhibit, lay bare, display or express something, whether emotion, Political interest and / or affiliation, or ones Faith.

The reality is, there can be perfect demonstrations of some things without congruence (agreement and consistency) Recently I say an politician on the television with two of his Party Loyal standing on either sides of him, and by the facial expressions of both men it was abundantly clear that they do not share his views, or agree with him on the points he demonstrated. A professional, who could either be an Actor, an Advertiser, A back –up- Singer or a musician, can and may perform excellently without any agreement or even liking, interest or devotion to the matter, but by engagement of others they may, and can do excellently.

The difference with today's call is, it is not a financial call, and it is not an engagement that has temporary rewards that may only last for a while, but it is a JESUS CALL, and the thing is he called before, and now he is calling again. There are many different calls and to many different people.

The book of Hebrews speaks to some heroes of faith from whom we can learn how to mature and be like, or be better than them, comparing ourselves with those heroes, the advantage that we have to be better than they, would be that we can bench mark them while most of them were initiator or pace setters.

Most success people, companies, organizations and countries are successful because they could stay aside and study the behaviors or performances of others, improve on their weaknesses and are able to become greater than their mentors.

Faith

Hebrews 11:06 "States that without it is impossible to please God."

He said to the woman in St. Luke 07:50 Woman thy faith has saved you, go in peace.

And in St. Luke 08: 23 – 27 he asked when the winds became boisterous he asked where is your faith?

St Matthew 08:05 – 13 the lepers could not be healed by the disciples as they had not demonstrated great faith, but what a difference it made when Jesus came,

St Matthew 17:19 -21 He said if our faith be as much as a mustard seed we can say to the mountains "remove hence to yonder place"

Ephesians 02: 08 "It is by Grace that we are saved through faith, and by ourselves" it is that faith that makes us believe that we will sit in heavenly places, because we are now united with Christ and the saints we will live in power and victory,

Ephesians 04:13 "Till we come in the unity of the faith and of the knowledge of the Son of God to a perfect man, unto the measure of the stature of the fullness of Christ."

The word call is mentioned

824 times in the English Bible,

529 times in the OT and

295 times in the NEW

Although not calls mentioned were directly made to God or by Him, but Dr. Luke and John to a lesser extent high light the Calls made by Jesus I want to expound on a few as follows

Nos.	Scriptures	What
1.	St. Luke 09:01	Jesus Call **the twelve** and gave them power and Authority over all devils and to cure diseases.
2.	St. Luke 08: 45 - 54	He brought the **damsel** back to life
3.	St. Luke 10:39	He called **Mary** and she sat at His feet
4.	St. Luke13:12	He called **the woman** and said: "Woman thou art Loose"
5.	St. Luke 15:06	He called **his friends** and said: "rejoice I have found my sheep which was lost.
6.	St. Luke 16:02	He called the **Rich man** and said: "give an account of your **stewardship.**" Are you paying your tithes?
7.	St. Luke 16:05	He called the **debtors** and asked How much do you owe?
8.	St. Luke18:16	He called the **disciples** and said: "Suffer the little children to come unto me"
9.	St. Luke 19: 05 - 10	He called **Zacchaeus**: "Make haste and come down for today salvation is come to your house"
10.	St. Luke 19: 12 - 29	He called the **10 servants** and gave them ten pounds and said occupy until I return
11.	St. John 01:48	He called **Nathaniel through Phillip**, so Nathaniel asked, "whence knows me, Jesus

		answered him before Phillip called you I saw you (an indirect call)
12.	St. John 12:17	He called **Lazarus** from the grave back to life.

Chapter 36
Behold He Calls Again

Reading Lesson Exodus 03: 01-10

"This discourse is about a low grade Job. A Shepherd's job in the Eastern land in those days paid very little. Moses was called from one low grade job to another". (He was call from a life of shepherding, to a life of leading God's people.) While Church Leadership, is similar in nature, to that of keeping sheep, they are both: "care giving and defending" they can both be classified as: "Servant Leadership" and in some cases the remuneration package may be small, the difference with the latter is that, no premium can be placed on the souls of men, because the scripture declares that a man's soul is priceless; and from that point of view; St. Matthew 16:26 says: "For what shall it profit a man if he shall gain the whole world, and loses his own soul? Or, what shall he give in exchange for his soul."

The word: "again" suggests that calls were made before, our stubbornness, our excuses, our lack of focus, sometimes put us in a state where we hesitate to answer someone's call, in the case of a call to ministry, we expect God to understand, but not so, the master work requires haste! Moses was quite comfortable tending his Father–In-Law's flock, while he had the support of his wife Zipporah, it may appear to us sometimes that, where we are at, is just where we ought to be, and nowhere else, and sometimes we can be so wrong.

A call is: A shout, or a loud cry, a call or a cry can, or may come from different sources or different persons, so it is important to know the caller voice, because if we don't know the caller very well, then we may very well ended up answering to the wrong caller, or neglecting an authentic call, or may even get involved with the wrong source. Sometime when calls are made whether for a schedule meal, to give attention to something or someone, or even to be attended to, we have the tendency to have persons waiting, until it becomes convenient to us, before we respond or even attempt to respond; I am sometimes inclined to think that it is bad manners.

In the event of God's call to Moses, he made four excuses, this lends to question to us: (how many have you made?)

1. In **Exodus 03:11** (He asked who am I?) Because he thought that he was personal unfit.
2. **Exodus 04:01** (He said: The people are going to doubt me) he suffered from the fears of unbelief by the people.
3. **Exodus 04:10** (He said, I am slow of speech & tongue, so I will not be able to communicate well with the people)
4. **Exodus 04:13** He requested that Aaron be sent instead of him.

Nb. We can learn from Moses' experience, not to put our own interests before the interest of God, because He can always do without us, but we can't do without Him. If we constantly make excuses, we will have to pay the penalty of disobedience, because God is a jealous God. And if we ignore His calls consistently, then He will burn our bushes to get our attention, so, even if we feel insufficient, or incapable to undertake a particular task, we need to understand that God is the source of all our resources. So he will always equip us for whatever task He gives us.

When God called Moses as we see in **Exodus 03:07** it was not about himself, it was about the Israelites in Egypt, Israel was in bondage and need to be delivered, our excuses and our low self esteem are not enough an excuse to make, once God calls us then he has a purpose for us, and everything else should take second place.

When God Called Abram

According to **Genesis 17: 01** Whenever God gives assignments he takes the responsibility to hold us accountable, he watches the way we walk, and listens the way we talk and discerns the attitude with which he carry out our assignments. He will even change our names and titles if the ones we carry do not represent the task He has in store for us. Example He changed Abram original name to Abraham, Jacob to Israel, and the list goes on; **Genesis 17:5-6**.

In the case of the Samuel's call, He called him three times but Samuel was still young and did not yet know the Lord, besides the word of the Lord was not yet revealed to him. So much so, that each time he heard the call he ran to Eli; Then, in **1st. Samuels 03: 10** He called his name twice and that was when he eventually answered. **Verses 4-8** but after he answered the call, God equip him for the task for which he was called, because Eli's house and his ministry were in trouble; and God wanted him to stand in that gap.

There are several other accounts that clearly suggest that we will have to make sacrifices in order to fulfill the call of God on our lives. In **Exodus 03: 20-22** it is recorded that "God called the Israelite women to a life of sacrifice, at this point in time, a gift was required from them (The Israelite women) they were to take with them into the land of Canaan: jewels of Gold and Silver, and they were to wear garments at a certain specification as well, but the women did not have what to give or what to wear, So God told the Israelite women to borrow the gold, the silver and the garments from the Egyptian women, and they should wear then into the land of Canaan, it was not only for them to look good, but more-so for them to take their spoils to fortify the Promise land. In Some cases we may be faced with situations where we may have to borrow to be able to fulfill our expected obligations, or may even have to borrow to assist others who maybe are in dire need, The Egyptians were using the gold and silver for the wrong reasons, (Belial Worship) God wanted them to look good, and not to worry about it, the plan was; if they die in the wilderness and didn't reach The land of Canaan alive, then   their children and the grandchildren would carry them to the promise land, if the Moses generation won't, or can't then the Joshua's generation will, and so it was; they would not leave the valuables in the wilderness, because they knew the importance of The Gold and the Silver, and the best part of it is, they would not have to repay the Egyptian women, and by that time however, both the borrower and the lender would have died, but the inherited legacy lives on, because both gold and silver are durable materials that can be pasted on from one generation to the next. If only we would follow the leading of the lord then the outcome will always be favorably. Try it!

Chapter 37
Be Careful Of Burnout

Introduction

To be burnt out is not just to suffer from exhaustion, or being used up, neither is it primarily the effects of too much hard work, or overworked, but in the true pastoral sense, it is more about losing the Anointing. It is very important to be able to discern the signs of a pastoral burnout. Because it is said by the experts that a pastor (for example can carry on his pastoral duties for as long as three years maximum) before his Ministry crumbles to the ground completely, because even though the Anointing leaves him or her, they can still use familiar procedures, coupled with years of experience and cruise on for a while, but will not be able to stand up under any significant pressure.

For instance if Pastors are only always giving, giving, giving, and never allow anyone to minister to, or pour into them, never take vacation, they will end up like an empty tank because all the fuel are all used up. So it can be compared to a vehicle runs out of petrol while going down a hill the momentum will take it all the way down to the bottom of the hill, depending on the state of the road it may continue on a flat surface, and maybe a little way on an incline, but will definitely not be able to go too far up the hill. Then the worst thing can happen if the vehicle is equip with Power Brakes, then with no power on, there is no braking mechanism to prevent it from rolling backwards, also if it is equip with a power steering, one may not be able to maneuver the vehicle from the possible dangers.

It is paramount that the ministers look after themselves, and spend quality time with their families, and rest. Rest is a discipline, and it is as necessary as work. And it should be factored in ones planning and scheduling for effectiveness. If leaders are going to teach and train other leaders then example is the best teacher.

Some of the behaviors that are usually displayed during the Burnout Period; are as follows:

- Hardly can anyone do anything to please the individual.
- They are always quick to find faults with the performances of others.
- They are always very quick to cast blame on others, (Pass on the buck).
- They become very thin-skinned and aggressive.
- They usually become judgmental.
- They are usually hard to please.
- They become Very defensive, and may even start lying in an effort to cover their tracks.
- The listening audience and the smart observers may detect that there is a disconnect between the leader and the followers, because we are Spiritual Beings, therefore when spirituality is lacking on the part of the Leader, then the outcome is usually obvious.

According to John Henderson's article (A Baptist Pastor) posted on Google, regarding Burnout. "He said numerous times per year, for as long as he can remember, he spoke with pastors who were looking for an exit from ministry. The reasons given were not moral failure, or interest in another vocation, or lack of "calling." The reason, more often than not, is nebulous and hard to describe. When the pastor talks about ministry, he uses words like, "exhausted, discouraged, pointless, distracted and lonely." No matter how much he sleeps, or drinks coffee, or tries to motivate himself, the tank always feels empty.

Is it this, what people call pastoral burnout? If so, how do we discern the signs? Answering that important question is the goal of this article.

Pastoral burnout could be defined as: "***The moment or season when a pastor loses the motivation, hope, energy, joy, and focus that is required to fulfill his work, and these losses usually impact the work itself.*** These aspects of burnout don't operate in isolation. They connect and overlap. From time to time, we might lose motivation or hope in ministry. On any given day, we can feel exhausted and joyless. But when all our motivations erode at once, and when their absence persists, I think it's *then* that we've entered a season of *pastoral burnout*. "

In my view the attitudes and behavior may not always be the same, but will vary from time to time, and from people to people, depending on the individual's temperament, and level of maturity coupled with academia (and by this I mean not perceived qualification, but certified, or formally approved qualifications, given through authentic sources, while credence is also paid to **QBE.)** (Qualified by Experience) I hereby refer to: Raymond Pruitt's Theology, founded in his book: "Fundamentals of the Faith" concerning the title ELDER, which has different shades of meaning: "The ordained ministry and those matured persons with a grown-up, yet growing relationship. (Maturity) See **1ˢᵗ. Timothy 03:01-07,** and **Titus 01:05-09.** And the Compact Dictionary of Doctrinal Word puts it this way: they are superior in wisdom and experience.

How to treat a burnout Minister.

There can be many different way to treat them, depending on the state of the Individual, regarding Age, Socio Economic status, family structure (which could include dependents) living condition and whether or not there are alternatives. Note though, that in realigning your beliefs. You should constantly remind yourself that God is in control,

1. May be a Sabbatical is the ideal.
2. Spend time with the Lord daily to find His will for your future...
3. Pray to God that the full effects of rest be realized.
4. Do introspection and reconciliation if necessary
5. Revitalize the Total Man.
6. Refreshing yourself in His Word and asking Him to lead and guide your decision.
7. Finding another field to serve in if that is the ideal.
8. Do Retraining.
9. Seek the Lord with all your strength, and be consistent in so doing,
10. Make hope in the Lord your Main Focus, and always remember that; it is patience that drives hope.

Conclusion

A burnout is not a death sentence. Neither is it an end, stepping aside voluntarily can be a noble move, (It is much better than have to be removed by rejection or by authority) when it is done out of a good conscience, it usually drives a more vigorous return, and a return with more confidence than if you were removed. Failure is the opportunity to do thing over and better. Therefore, we can always learn from the mistakes of others, rather than have to make them ourselves.

Finally if within our introspection, a burnout steers us in the face, rather than stay for the purpose of maintaining ones pride, and end up with a fall I suggest step aside or take Sabbatical that will save ourselves and also save others, It is better to be safe than to be sorry.

Think seriously.

God Bless.

Chapter 38
Religious Exploitation; Be Careful!

Exploitation: Is defined as: Mistreatment meted out to someone expecting personal gains in return, utilization of another person for selfish reason, using someone over whom you may have authority, management, abuse or operation regarding persons under one's control, services which could be better and fairly utilized for the good of both parties, this can be in the religious or secular field, in whichever category it is used, it is out of place for Christians and especially for Religious Leaders. All forms of mistreatment should be avoided by upright citizens, but is out of place for leaders. To be religious is to be sacred, holy, devote, pious and dutiful. All the definitions of the word, righteousness are related to uprightness, hence there should always be associated with the Religious, while the word exploitation should not be closely related to the righteous, but sad to say unscrupulous (corrupt, dishonest, crooked, men have crept in the flock, and sometimes gain prominence and has so influenced others, because behaviour is learnt.

According to **Jude 01:04** "For there are certain men crept in unawares, who were before of old ordained to condemnation, ungodly men turning the grace of God into lasciviousness, and denying the only Lord God, and our Lord Jesus Christ." Jude wrote this to the Jewish Christian brethren from as far back as A.D. 65 to warn the Church of the unscrupulous men, they are still here today and among us therefore we have to take this warning seriously, because those men are serious in their pursuit to establish heresy among us; because they are false teachers and leaders who reject the Lordship of Christ undermined the faith of others and lead them astray, state clearly that: These leaders and any who follow them will surely be punished. Apostasy and rebellion against God are punishable, so we are to avoid drifting away from a faithful commitment to God.

Leaders and aspirants are to treat with importance, and practice a staunch defense of the Christian faith, and avoid anyone who distorts the Bible to suit their own purpose, but stand up and defend Christ, and portray Him in words and conduct.

Jude, when compared to the other books of the Bible said the least, but it is enough to help us to escape the terrible punishment that is reserved for all those who violates the Teachings of Christ. So neither should we be subjected to exploitation or be inclined to exploit anyone.

Jude pointed out that as servants of Jesus: mercy, peace and love should be shared in abundance. In Theology the Latin word: Sub; which means under and ordinaries: and suggest the Father and Son, which subordinates the Son to the Father, yet in essence and stature it endangers the son's divinity, but is liken to the equal power of the trinity, while equality does not really mean sameness, each person deserves to get what is rightfully theirs and be treated fairly. Insubordination, in some circles is viewed as an unwelcome word in some circles of society and even in the modern church, the true definition of the word is: "disobedience, defiance, rebelliousness, unruliness, and noncompliance." And even some religious commentators, according to four of the New Testament reference those points vividly to masters and servants according to:

1. **1ˢᵗ. Peter 02:18** "Servants, be subject to your masters with fear, not only to the good and gentle, but also to the forward.
2. **Titus 02:09** "Exhort servants to be obedient unto their own masters, and to please them well in all things; not answering again."

3. **Ephesians 06:05** "Servants, be obedient to them that are your masters according to the flesh, with fear and trembling, in singleness of your heart, as unto Christ."

4. **Colossians 04:01** "Masters provide your slaves with what is right and fair, because you know that you also have a Master in heaven"

Some commentators believe the whole matter of slavery is to be condemned, the NIV puts it this way according to Colossians 04:01. That Paul was maybe speaking to Philemon who was a Slave owner in the Colossian Church; and Onesimus was his slave. (In fact a run-a-way slave) he did not condemn slavery then because slavery was very common practice in the Roman Empire, and evidently some Christians had slaves then, but he made it clear the slave Onesimus and the slave owner Philemon are brothers in Christ, and should be treated as such. **Philemon 01:15, 16** The Commentary states that: Slavery was so widespread in the Roman Empire then, and the Christians did not have the Political power to change the slavery system then, it was later on that the gospel began to change the Social structures by changing the people within it. So, when it was finally changed then Philemon and Onesimus were no more master and slave but brothers in Christ.

Here it is that if life is kind to us and our brothers or sisters did not enjoy equal opportunities and if we are in a position to employ others, or supervise them, then we should treat each other well; if we occupy leadership positions in the church it doesn't make lord over others **St. John 13:16** "Jesus said unto you The servant is not greater than his lord, neither is the lord. Neither is he that is sent greater than he that sent him. V17 "If he know these things, Happy are ye if ye do them." These are the direct words of Jesus.

In that exploitation comes in various forms; it may be good to highlight these for vigilance and a greater focus, with the hope that going forward these will be avoided.

Below is a table of some of the types of exploitations; in my view some of them are done frequently, with full knowledge of the outcome, while others may be done unwittingly.

#s	Exploiters	Exploited
1	Ministers of Religion (Pastors)	Members of a Fellowship (Laity)
2	Ministers of Government (Politicians)	Citizens
3	Land lords	Tenants
4	Employers	Employees
5	Lenders	Borrowers
6	Sponsors	Beneficiaries
7	Drivers	Passengers
8	Sellers	Buyers
9	The Rich	The Poor
10	The powerful	The Vulnerable

May we all do some introspection here and now and treat with urgency, any situation of exploitation, even the resemblance of it. So that we will not cause any to stumble or stand in the ways of anyone but be clear when we speak, and clearer in how we live.

Blessings.

Chapter 40
Yielding Fully To The Master's Call

Scripture Reading: 2nd Chronicles   30:- 07 - 08

I will use four key words from the Theme, to assist me in bringing my point across. They are: Yielding, Fully. Master and Call.

Yielding: Being soft, like Elastic, being squashy

Fully: Totally, completely, copious.

Master: Is a person having control, like the captain of a merchant ship, the owner of a slave, or an animal, one who holds or gets the upper hand of another, or, of something, such as the holder of a University Degree. So if you are a master, it means that you are an authority.

Call: A Call is a Shout, a loud cry, it can come from different Persons, or from different sources, So, it is important to know the *CALLER* if we don't know the caller very well, then we may end up answering to the wrong caller / and then get involved with the wrong source. A call is sometimes done as an approval or a bidding of someone mostly in authority, like in a game of cricket it is usually done by the umpire; to approve or disallow an appeal.

A **call** is usually made by a clergyman with an urgent appeal, it can also be done to ward off someone from impending danger, or to return by the way one came. ***But there is also a point of no return.*** (This is usually done because of expiration; by date, by mercy or by season) but the wise man Solomon said in **Ecclesiastes Chapter 03** "that there is a time for everything under the sun"

I'll Quote **Zechariah 01:04** "Be ye not like your fathers, unto whom the former prophets have cried, saying thus saith the Lord of host, turn ye now from your evil ways, and from your evil doings: but they did not hear, nor harkens unto me saith the Lord. **V5** Your father's where are they? And the prophets, do they live forever?

Lord. According to the Dictionary of Doctrinal Words the word: Lord (from the Anglo Saxon Halfords is the "Bread Keeper" the one who has power and authority over others and in the OT is translated as Yahweh, Jehovah as a name for God,   and for Christ the son of God, **1ˢᵗ Corinthians 08:06** states that "He is the only one, and through Him all things exist."

Read Psalm 145: 18 -21 (Speaks of A divine nearness to the obedient) When David said that the Lord is Nigh to those that call upon Him, we know that there is no distance with Him because He is Omnipresent, rather He spoke of relationship that is beyond convenience, once you have the call of God on your life, there is a compulsion laid upon you and you just have to be always available to the master's will. This goes both ways because not only that His call imposes on us the demand for duties; He yields to our desires and our cries, whether for help, deliverance' sustenance and, or to save. And not just for a short period of time but forever and ever.

When a call is made, whether for a schedule meal or for some other things, some of us have a tendency to have persons waiting, until it become convenient to us, before we respond, or even attempt to, I sometimes believe it is bad manners.

The Moses' Call

One prime example of an important call was, the Moses Call according to: **Exodus 03: 01 – 10**

In the event when He called Moses, he made four excuses, (how many have you made?).

1. Personal Unfitness. **Exodus 03:11** (Who am I)
2. Fears and unbelief of the people. **Exodus 04: 01** (They are going to doubt me)
3. Lack of Eloquence. **Exodus 04:10.** (I am slow of speech and tongue)
4. Request that Aaron be sent instead as an alternative leader. **Exodus 04:13**

When God place a call on someone's life, He or She may run, but they cannot hide; and if we continue to run He will burn our bushes to get our attention, like He burnt Moses' to get his attention. A God Call is a different call, because most times it is not so much about you, as it is about others. **Exodus 03: 07** States, **t**hat Moses call was not primarily about him as it was about the Israelites in Egypt, he could not be selfish and got away with it, while Israel was in bondage and needed to be delivered, our excuses and our low self esteem are not enough excuses to make, while the Master select us for duty.

The Abraham's Call

Genesis 17: 01 When someone calls you, usually they watch your overall response, but especially the way you walk, in the event of Abram he walked crookedly, then God said to him V.01: "I am the Almighty God, Walk before me and be thou perfect".

When our ways please Him He will change your name like Abraham, (from Abram to Abraham) some of us have a bad name and are badly in need of a change., because the ones we have now does not represent well the Church we are suppose to represent.

The Samuel's Call

In the case of Samuel's call according to **1st Samuel 03: 04-10**

Vs. 04-08 - Once He called him three times

V.10 - He gave him a repeat call (Samuel, Samuel) that is a serious matter, when special emphasis has to be place on your call, but that was when he answered.

Vs. 21 – 22 - States that God is calling us to sacrifice, He told the Israelite women (who did not have what to give as sacrifice) to go and borrow from the Egyptian their gold and their silver to build up Canaan. Canaan could use it for the right reason while they are not using it for the right reason, when you borrow their gold and their silver, don't worry about it. Even if you should die in the wilderness, and you don't reach the promise land with it, then your children will and your grand children will carry them to the land of Canaan, if the Moses generation won't, then the Joshua's Generation certainly will.

However, once we are called, the best thing to do is to answer, and to answer promptly, because we may not be as fortunate as Samuel, to receive the repeat call and several others. Some of us may only be called once. Today the Saviour call! Answer now, will You?

Chapter 41
Maximized The Blessing That Unity Brings

There is tremendous amount of blessing available to us, but there are certain conditions that must first be met before they can be realized, example "unity" Psalm 133:01-03 states: "behold how good and how pleasant it is for brethren to dwell together in unity. It is like the precious oil upon the head running down on the beard, the beard of Aaron; running down to the edge of his garment. It is like the dew of Harmon, descending upon the mountains of Zion. For there the Lord commanded the blessing, even life forevermore.

Unity is defined by the Oxford Dictionary as: Agreement, accord, concord. The Psalmist David puts it this way: unity is pleasant and precious, unfortunately, it does not always abound in the Church as it should, and people disagree and cause division over unimportant issues, some members delight in causing tension by disagreeing with others. Unity is in the church is crucial:

1. It makes the church a positive example to the world, and help in drawing others to us.
2. It helps the body of believers to corporate in the manner that Christ intended it to be.
3. It renews and vitalizes the body by sapping up the energies that usually caused tension among persons. Living is unity does not means that we agree on everything, there will be many opinions, similar to the many notes in a musical Chord, however we must agree on our purpose in life which is to: work together in unity for God, which usually reflect our inward unity of purpose.

Moses used the expensive oil to anoint Aaron as the first High Priests of Israel, and to dedicate all the other priests to God's service, like the anointing oil, brotherly unity shows that we are dedicated to serving God wholeheartedly, according to **Exodus 29:07**. Mt. Hermon is the tallest mountain in Palestine and it is located north of the sea of Galilee.

To further highlight the point that unity brings success, is the story of the two boys on the rail line, individually it was very difficult to walk on the rail line; it was something you could not do for long if you are walking by yourself, because it was too slippery and also very narrow, so the two brothers held hands and walked together, they were able to do it for miles without falling off it, because it give balance and supports the other, so because of unity they were able to walk for miles.

Paul in his statement to the Roman, compared the church to the human body and the activities that is to be carried out by the different individuals, **Romans 13: 04-05** he also said to the Ephesians in **chapter 04: 03, 13** he said: harmony is not usually achieved all at once rather it is a gradual process which must be approached accordingly, in this we need to be **more** tolerant of each other, even though our views on various subjects may be different as compared to how the musical chords though different, yet they complement each others.

To the Philippians Paul said: "Whatever happens, conduct yourselves in a manner worthy of the gospel of Christ so that whether I come and see you or I hear about you; I will know that your stand firm in the spirit, contending as one man for the faith of the gospel and be not frightened by those who oppose you. the Apostle Peter also said in **1st Peter 03:08** There is an enjoined unity that speak of all of us being one having the same mind, having compassion one for another, love as brethren and be pitiful and courageous, not rendering evil for evil or railing for railing, but contrariwise blessings, knowing that ye are therefore called, that ye should receive a blessing.

There are persons who share the same space but have different views on certain points Matthew states, that this behavior is usually driven by traditions or inner peace. the Scribes and the Pharisees of the day were overly concerned about the washing of the hands, more that obeying the Laws of God regarding authority; which includes parents, governmental and divine authorities; **St. Matthew 15:04** says: "anyone who curse father and mother should be put to death" those were strong rules regarding the respect for parents.

Unity is not only external but is also internal, our hearts and our lips should always agree, because if unity is lacking internally there is going to be confusion, and in most cases it can be seen by others; therefore unity extends I far beyond just members of the family or the same organization, or citizens of a country. It is not enough to speak about unity or to act religious, our actions and our worship must be sincere, and an example of how the Pharisees knew a lot about Jesus, but did not know him personally they were blind to the truth of God. Jesus told the people, "don't let them lead you it is like blind leading the blind you will both fall into the ditch. Today people study religious history, and are very good at it; but the best way to know Jesus is to know Him personally.

Conclusion

As we read this material, I encourage you as In take courage for myself to make sure that our attitudes in whole resembles Jesus and not the Scribes and the Pharisees, and if any behavior of the unbecoming, then let this be the moment of truth when we do introspection and make all adjustment to our lives to be fully in line with divine which is in Christ Jesus. when this is done then, those of the contrary path will make the right move, wanting to

be like Jesus and will be enthused to become Christians like us and stay in line with Paul's instruction, "Follow me as I follow Christ."

Chapter 42
Things And Times Have Changed, God Does Not

When people get accustomed and comfortable doing things a certain way, and all of a sudden things changes and get out of control, such as dressing, grooming, socializing, worshipping travelling and doing business in a certain way, then everything changes, it can become so bothersome to us to effect all the changes and become comfortable again.

Heraclitus: "A Greek Philosopher said: Change is the only constant in life"

Change, like season, do occur, life and people change too, when all efforts are made to get things the way you want them, and then something happen beyond your control, you may lose your friends, the way you learnt to do things are no longer relevant; and it is like starting life all over again.

It is at this point that the Prayer of serenity comes into play:

> "God grant me the serenity,
> to accept the things I cannot change,
> the courage to change the things I can,
> and the wisdom to know the difference"

Our humanness and the ability to govern ourselves all come to show the level of inconsistencies that are in us, but there is one who is superior to us in everything and that is Jesus, one thing to note just a few months ago one would not be allowed to enter a band wearing a mask, would be stopped by the security officers, and if one deer to put up resistance you would be treated harshly. Today Life's tables has turn, it is like a brand new world; the paradigm has shifted, and things seems like a brand new world, and we have to find new and innovative ways to do things.

With the unchanging characteristics of the Almighty, we need to understand some standards that will not change regardless:

His Immutability (For I am the Lord I change not, therefore the sons of Jacob are not consumes) **Malachi 03:06**

Divine Constancy (From everlasting to everlasting; Thou are God) **Psalm 90:02**

Divine Compassion (It is the Lord's mercy why we are not consumed, because his compassion fails not, they are new every morning; great is Thy faithfulness) **Lamentation o3:22-23**

Hospitality (Especially as it relates to our social duties to our fellowmen, especially the less fortunate and the vulnerable among us. Jesus is the same yesterday, today and forever) **Hebrews 13: 08**

Therefore we must all seek tom be like Jesus, being consistent in our good traits, and Christian lifestyle, because change can be very noticeable, it caused Jeremiah to cry, (today he is known as the weeping prophet) **Lamentation 04:01** "How is the gold become dim, how is the fine gold changed? The stone of the sanctuary are poured out on top of each street" **About 586 B.C.** Jerusalem the fenced city was taken siege by their Babylonian counterpart while the natives had to stay inside and suffer needs while their enemies had more than enough of their goods to lavish, all because of the sins of the people, God's anger was also great because it should not have been that way.

We need to know not to glory in prosperity, because if expectation changes for the worst then the repercussion can be great also. **Romans**

05:20 states that: Where sin abounded, grace did much more abound, therefore it took much grace for them to even endure that hardship. Paul said in **2nd. Corinthians 09: 08** "God is able to make all grace abound (be plentiful) toward you, that ye, always having all sufficiency in all things, may abound to every good works., again Paul told the Philippians in Chapter 01:09 "I pray that your love may abound yet more and more in knowledge and in all judgment.

I am sure that the Christians were not worst off during this COVID-19 period because the word of God comes alive and the scriptures are fulfilled: "In times of famine, my people shall be satisfied" even during this period many Christians had more than enough, and were able to share with others, we don't k now what tomorrow will bring , but for now. Thankfully, God is to be praised. Even though we do not know what tomorrow holds, we just need to ask God to order our st.eps and everything will be okay.

It is enough to know that our God changes not, and his words will not pass, because He is a faithful God, he is faithful to thousands of generations, and b e cause of the unchanging character of the Almighty, we can rest securely in the promise of the Lord, concerning the happy state of the Godly Psalm 37:25-26 : " I have been young now I am old, yet I have never seen the righteous forsaken, nor his seed begging bread. He is merciful, and lendeth, and his seed is blessed.

Chapter 43
Our Final Move

The certainties of death struck from time to time in our individual families in a way that, no matter how one thinks he or she is prepared for such event, we sometimes find out that we are dead wrong, although we all know that death is the one appointment that we must keep, regardless of how good, or punctual a person we are, and even if we are only a junk, it make only little difference, we sometimes don't know when or where for sure, but death just steps into our families and take away our loved ones, with no intention to give them back to us, at least not in this life.

Jesus said in His words as is written in **Hosea 13:14** "I will ransom them from the powers of the grave; I will redeem them from death, I will be thy plagues oh death I will be thy destruction". The only power that has ever, or will be able to overcome the power of death is the resurrection.

Today I quote from **Proverbs 01:08**: "My son forsake not the law of thy mother" and **15:20**: "It is only a foolish son that despised his mother" and liken God's love to that of a mother and a baby.

Mothers were created not only to fulfill the household and domestic duties associated with child rearing, but more-so for the shaping of their lives for the cause of God, in fulfilling high and holy duties, which are of greater importance than being the nurse, the good cook, the hair dresser, and stylist, the teacher among other good traits, but the mother who leads by example, a Godly life far exceed all the heights that great men reached and kept.

I call on the fathers to take their responsibility as priest of our house hold very seriously, knowing it is not only to be provider and protector for our family, but above everything else, we are to lead the charge of being an example to our family and set the rules by which the family is to be guided, and say like Joshua in **Chapter 24:15** "As for me and my house we will serve the lord" there is no guarantee that the rules will be upheld after the children become adults and leave the home, however our duty still stands, we would have played our part.

I call on everyone who reads this discourse, thinking that almost every family would have had at least one bereavement experience at some point in their lives, also let us reflect on how much worst and hurtful the death of a loved one can be, if according to our assessment of the life of the deceased, there is not enough to celebrate, and their dreams were not fulfilled.   That is more than enough to caused us, grief and sorrow, there is a great difference when we can cherished the grand hope that the Christian journey offers.

I use this opportunity to call us to a more assertive and excellent lifestyle and seek to encourage us to pay greater attention to an urgent call for all to make the decisions regarding our eternal destiny, my friends the day of death is here, and we are all dying, but Jesus said "I am come that ye might have life and have it more abundantly.

The late Dr. Billy Graham wrote in his book: "Death and the After Life" If we know in advance the moment we are going to die, then most of us would order our lives differently, also note carefully that we have to our disposal various programs that can assist us in living longer; these include: fitness programs, dietary programs, new cholesterol control programs, weight control programs, exercise equipment with many others not mentioned. These can certainly add years to life, but no cure has been found for death, so people are still dying, and we are all on death row.

My sisters and brothers, let us be ready for there is a time for everything under the sun the wise man Solomon said, in that we have no control over some of the thing in life, such as our life span, our health among some other things, let us do the things that we have control over, and make sure that we are prepared for our final move from this life. It is appointed unto man once to die, and after death comes the judgment. So let us all be prepared, getting ready is not an option, but a deliberate action, it is a choice, and choices come with responsibility therefore we certainly will reap whatever we have sown.

Conclusion

There are two moving allegations concerning death and taxes, they are not escaped easily, yet it is said, that with the right accountant at work we can avoid paying any taxes at all, but to date no cure has been found for death. If that was so some rich men and women around us would not have died, but until then we are all on death row and daily we are dying. Death it is not altogether a bad thing, it can also be a form of healing, or deliverance from some things. One thing I know it is not reversible and renders mankind powerless, therefore anything we need to do for ourselves or others, it is recommended that we do it now (in fact, do it today) because life may not be as kind to us tomorrow, as it is today.

"Let us make ourselves ready for the final move!"

Section 3
Social Issues For All Sectors Of Society

Chapter 44
Only The Righteous Shall Inherit The Earth

This is the direct writing of Paul as he wrote to the Roman brethren regarding the Gospel which is given to all men for Justification through faith, **he** wrote in: **Romans 01:16-20.** "He said, he was not ashamed of the gospel of Jesus Christ, for it was the power of God unto salvation to everyone that believeth; both Jews and Greek, and further state that the just shall live by faith, by the righteousness of God that is revealed from faith to faith. It is important to note that God's wrath is revealed from Heaven against all ungodliness and the unrighteousness of men, to which there is no excuse".

Righteousness is described by: The Compact Dictionary of Doctrinal Words as follows: "Something is righteous if it agrees with the divine or moral law, and is free from guilt or sin. It further states, that the righteousness of God, however, is more than fulfilling an external code of what is right: It is an attribute of God's very nature, because God does not arbitrarily decide what is right or wrong, good or bad; rather, righteousness and goodness flows out of the character of God himself according to **Romans 04: 3, 24"**

Therefore no one can be righteous or godly without the very attribute of God is reveals to him, fully, and a dependency on His mercy is accessed through a submission of the human nature, to His divine nature; according to **Romans 04:05 which** says: "But to him that worketh not, but believe on him that justifies the ungodly, his faith is counted for righteousness. So. It is clear that it is not of works, that we have done, it is the gift of God.

Inherit: To inherit something as it is defined by: **The New Compact Bible Dictionary,** more relates to families rather than to individuals, and relates more to land, estate and other properties than anything else. That something should remain in the family and should not be sold. It further states that in the Mosaic law, only the sons of a legal wife had rights to inheritance, for the firstborn son possessed the birthright, and is entitled to a double portion of the father's possession, and to him belong the duty of maintaining the females of the family according to: **Deuteronomy 21:15-17.** Only if there were no sons then the property could be given to the daughter according to **Numbers 27:08** (only if they were married in their own tribe) if the widow remarries then the land would be passed on to a male near next of kin on the side of the deceased husband. (So, if she wants to retain it, then she would have to remain unmarried. (An example of an inheritance is Abraham and the land of Canaan, **"concerning the** divine favor to his seed; the Israelites."** According to **(1st. Kings 08:36)**

The story of the two sons mentioned in **St. Luke 15:11-32 The** younger son **(the Prodigal)** took his portion, went into the far country, where he wasted it then he returned to enjoy what should rightfully be for the older son (his brother) it cost resentment, and resistance by the older son, because in principle, he is entitled to twice the portion of the younger son, and for him to have wasted his portion, then return enjoyed a part of his older brother's portion, it was both unreasonable, unfair because it was a reversal of the Jewish tradition, that is why it caused resentment, but a father's love goes beyond reason, beyond tradition, beyond fairness and may sometimes reaches the heights beyond reason, beyond fairness, and beyond tradition to a point beyond perceived love, to the realm of mercy; which is one of the components of true love, because true love keeps no record of wrongs, but is patient, is kind and is forgiving, and aims to fulfill a purpose. Purpose usually rises above criticism, because it know no shame, and sometimes revolutionizes polices, principles, culture and procedures just to give someone, another opportunity to get it right; For greater love have no man than this, that a man lay down his life for his friend. for while we were yet sinners; Christ died for us.

Earth: "Is this planet on which we live, although it has a variety of meanings, including a material substance, a territory it is even referred to as: inhabitance of world." All this and more we will inherit, because the promise to inherit the earth, or eternal life, starts the moment we accepts Christ. And last through the ages.

Through Christ redemptive work, we have received an inheritance by adoption to become heirs of God and joint-heirs with Jesus, according to **Romans 08:17** which points to: A guaranteed eternal inheritance given to us through the Holy Spirit. **Ephesians 01:14** reads: "Which is the earnest of our inheritance until the redemption of the purchased possession, unto the praise of His glory. (Which is a spiritual Inheritance) and that is the only way we Gentiles accessed the entitlement to inherit that which is allotted to the righteous, and the righteous only. Not of works, that we should boast. It is the gift of God. So let us not blow it, like easy come, or never see, come see! So let us be grateful and appreciative to Christ, for His death on the cross of Calvary, for us.

Conclusion:

In the Epistle to the Hebrews, Paul said: "As Israel in the Old Covenant, received her inheritance from God. So in the New Covenant, the New Israel receives inheritance, which is not for Jews only, but includes all believers, including the Gentiles, this inheritance in the kingdom with all its blessings, both present and **eschatological**, are God's gift to mankind. (Which in Theology, is the last things, things associated with the beliefs regarding the final things such as death, immortality, Judgment day, heaven and hell, the end of the earth and the end of human history.) It is also not designed to satisfy

181

curiosity, but to provide an intelligent comprehension of the future things, as a guide for present programs; and is a sure ground for hope, and is unlike the hopes that the fragmented world offers to heathens. It is wholly the gift of God's sovereign Grace, for the righteous, even though it is offered to all.

> So I'll quote the song: "I am Amazed"
> "I am amazed that He loves me.
> I am amazed that he you cares.
> Through your precious blood I am pardoned
> All my Sins are all washed away."

In that he loves us so much, let us love Him too, as the scripture says: "If you love me, keep my commandments.

May God bless you All.

Chapter 45
Redeeming The Time

Read: Geneses 17: 01-08 (Abraham)

Abraham: The son of Terah, the Father of the Chosen family,

1. He was called the Father of the Faithful
2. He was obedient (He left home and friends at the call of God **Geneses 12:04**
3. He was unselfish, he gave Lot the first choice of the land **13:09**
4. He was courageous, he defeated the robber kings **14:14**
5. He was benevolent, he gave tithes to Melchizedek the priest **14:20**
6. He was also incorruptible, he refused to accept gifts for service rendered to (the king of Sodom offered him a trade off bout he refuse) **14:23**
7. He was also mighty in prayer (While in Sodom he prayed to God and asked for favour not to destroy the righteous with the wicked and God answered his prayer) **18:23-33**
8. Most of all he was wonderful in faith, he was willing to offer up his only son Isaac **Hebrew 11:17**

Note carefully that as strong and faithful as Abraham was he distorted the truth under direct pressure with Sarah his (wife) his half sister (Terah's daughter) that was a common practice in those days, if a man's wife was not fruitful, then the unfruitful wife could decide to ask another woman to bear a child for her, with her husband, after which the original wife would adopt the child; Sarah did that to her husband, with Hagar because they were passed age, it later caused her embarrassment and pain, because made them a promise. Time is important, when God says He is going to, or has done something, we just need to be patient because His words are always sure,

With Abraham and Sarah, the plan seemed harmless to Abraham at the time yet, one can just imagine how many times Sarah regretted engaging Hagar so intimately in her life, and more so in her marriage, had she known that it would come to haunt her, then most likely she would not have traded her embarrassment, doubts and impulse for the satisfaction for her pride and impatience. Certainly she paid a price far above that which they bargained for, or could have even imagined. The relationship between Sarah and Hagar became bitter after Hagar got pregnant, so much so that Hagar started to mock Sarah, because Abraham started to pay more attention to Hagar (the young maid) it caused a great degree of jealousy between Sarah and Hagar, so Sarah complained to Abraham Genesis 16:05 then Abraham replied: "Your maiden is in your hand; do to her whatever you think best" in resonse to that Sarah mistreated Hagar and she ran away. **Genesis 16:06.**

Ephesians 05:15 -20 Paul warns us to be careful, due to the times we are living, that by all means we are to acknowledge that the days are evil; we can now learn from the mistakes of Abraham and Sarah; concerning their surrogate child (Ishmael) according to Genesis 16:15; There is no right way to do the wrong thing, the right thing is, to wait on the Lord: "But they that wait upon the Lord shall renew their strength, they shall mount up with wings as the eagles, they shall run and not be weary; and they shall walk and not faint"

Some things in life requires haste, other things require patience, when it comes to waiting on the Lord, patience is quite in order, when it comes to making the decision concerning things of great value, then patience is the ideal, however concerning pending danger then haste is in order, of all the options that are available to us the Master's work requires haste. There is a warning in **Ecclesiastes 07:09** "Be not hasty in thy spirit to be angry for anger resteth in the bosom of fools, let us be patient and wait on the lord, because He promised to strengthen our hearts, more so the time in which we live requires it.

Chapter 46
Is It difficult To Love, And If Yes, Why?

Love in Christian Theology is defined by the Dictionary of Doctrinal Words as follows: The ability to love is a vital aspect of being created in God's image and are regenerated by the Holy Spirit's Power; according to **1st. John 04 :07-11** "Beloved, let us love one and other, for love is from God. And everyone who loves is born of God and knows God." And anyone who does not love does not know God, for God is love. But His words declare: Beloved: if God so love us, we ought to love one another. By this the love of God was manifested in us. In that God has sent His only begotten son into the world so that the word through Him might live through Him. In this is love, not that we love God, but that He love us and sent His Son to be the propitiation for our sins. So we ought to love one and other.

Love is one of God's most important attributes. Four of the most common Greek words for love are:

1. **Philia:** Usually translated "friendship," "tender affection";
2. **Eros:** Which usually refers to sexual or physical passion, but was never used in the New Testament
3. **Storge:** "Family affection" this was also not used in the New Testament.
4. **Agape:** Which is best defined as "Intelligently, intentionally willing the best for each other, it is the attitude of God toward His son and toward us. According to **St. John 03:16** and Romans 05:08.

Further to other schools of thought, regarding the definition of the word Love; the New Compact Bible Dictionary defines it this way: it is the greatest of the Christian virtues, and takes its definition from the Holy Scriptures. It also said that "All human love, whether God ward or manward has its source in God. Love in its true reality and power is seen only in the light of Calvary 1st. **John 04:07-10** It is created in the believer by the Holy Spirit, prompting him to love both God and man, and finds it expression in service to our fellowmen; which is the chief test of Christian discipleship, according to **St. John 03:14.** Which require the Christians to love God supremely and his fellowmen as himself. It is also required of us to our enemy as our brother, and this must be without Hypocrisy, because LOVE is the bond uniting all the Christian virtues. **Colossians 03:14.** And concludes that Love lies at the very heart of Christianity, being essential to man's relationship to God and man.

The word LOVE is found 574 times in the English Bible: 300 times in the Old Testament and 274 times in the New Testament. It is more commonly written and so often times read, than is being practiced, yet we still wonder: "why is it so difficult to do. It is clear that different people love different things example the Genesis account in chapter 25: 28 "And Isaac loved Esau, because he did eat of his venison; but Rebekah love Jacob" look at the fact that Esau and Jacob were brothers and they were also twins, but obviously they were both of the same parents but were different in appearance.; verse 25 states that Esau was red and his skin was like a hairy garment, while Jacob was smooth skin. Sometimes our choice to love something or someone is driven by what meets the eye. But Jesus wants us to love without dissimulation, and the Apostle Paul said in **Romans 12:09:** "Let love be without dissimulation, abhor that which is evil; cleave to that which is good." Obviously Jacob and Esau were loved because of their appearances, which was driven primarily by the racial connections over which the children had no control. Sometime the choices we make to love or to hate are done by misguided choices; also we become victims of similar circumstances which are driven by the way we are seen or by the lenses that we are seen through. Therefore I always say our humanness will cause us to err. And in light of the scripture in we do not always get in right. So one of my favorite scriptures is **Jeremiah 10:23-24** "O Lord, I know that the ways of man is not in himself, it is not in man that walketh to direct his steps. O Lord correct me, but with judgment and not with Thine anger, lest Thou bring me to judgment."

Our dependence should always be in God, because distance lends enchantment to the view, and once we make our decisions based only on what we see, we will most times realized that the glittering and the golden images that capture our attention turn out to be more disastrous than anything; it happens in the choices some people make with their career, where they choose to leave the church they attend, and even the life partner they choose, because when we realize later on things turn, not the way we anticipate, and other times the opposite to our expectations.

Genuine Love, not perceived love, doeth no ill to its neighbour, is kind and keeps no record of wrongs, rather is kind and forgiving, and does not hesitate to tell those we love that they are wrong, whenever they are, but with a good attitude do, so the person can get back in the right alignment.

It is paramount that we carefully compare and contrast the two words: "Love and hate" in order to make the right choice, because they give opposite rewards. While the word LOVE is found **574** times in the English Bible: **300** times in the Old Testament and **274** times in the New Testament; the word HATE also appears **179** times in the English Bible as well; with **141** times in the Old Testament and **38** times in the New Testament. I am glad that a greater weight is laid on the word love more that it is on the word hate. Hate is defined by the English Dictionary as: extreme dislike, disgust and detestation, which are all the opposite meaning of the word love, and **St. Matthew 05:43** clear differentiation as to how they should be applied. **V.43** "Ye have heard that it has been said. Thou shall love thy neighbour, and hate thine enemy." So while that is said (that the Christian love should be enjoined, and the Enemies should be despised) Jesus said in **V.44-48** "But I say unto you, love your enemies, bless them that curse you, do good to them that hate you, and pray for them which despitefully use you and persecute you, because God makes the sun to shine on the evil and on the good, and sends rain on the just and on the unjust, for if you love only those who love you, what reward have ye? because that is what the publicans do; so salute them likewise, don't only do good to the brethren. Be ye therefore perfect, even as your heavenly Father is perfect.

Jesus also said in **St. John 15:18-20**: They hated me before they hate you, and the servant is not greater than his Lord, so if they hated and persecuted me then they will do the same to you; and note this, that Jesus said they hated Him with a cause. Hating the Christians is usually by the enemies and not by the Christians, what we are instructed to hate is wrongs. Paul further said to the **Hebrews** in Chapter **01:09-10** "Thou hath love righteousness, and hate iniquity, therefore God, even thy God hath anointed thee with the oil of gladness above thy fellows, and that the Lord has laid the foundation of the earth and the heaven from the beginning and they are the works of His hand. In **Psalm 110:03-06** He said: "For we ourselves were sometimes foolish, disobedient, deceived and serving divers lusts and pleasures, living in malice and envy, hatred and hating one and other, but after the kindness and love of God our Saviour toward man appeared. Not of righteousness which we have done, but according to His mercy He saved us by the washing of regeneration and renewing of the Holy Ghost, which He shed on us abundantly through Jesus Christ our saviour.

Conclusion

So unless, and until our hearts are regenerated by the blood of Jesus, we really don't know how to love, for LOVE is of God. 1st. John 04:20-22 says: "If a man say he love God and hateth his brother he is a liar, for he that loveth not his brother whom he hath seen, how can he love God whom he hath not seen. And this commandement have we from Him that he who loves God loves his brother also."

Love You Lots.

Chapter 47
Stay Focus And Don't Be A Drifter

Read Genesis 19:23–29

Gives an account of Abram and his nephew Lot who, even though Lot did not pay enough respect towards his uncle Abram, regarding the customs and cultures of the day; bearing in mind that it was Abram who received the promise and was more deserving of his father Terah's wealth, because being the son of Terah, he was the one who was the heir to his father's estate, while Lot was a little farther away from the inheritance; and should have waited his turn, but he was both disrespectful and impatient.

2nd. Peter 02:09–18

Speaks of: How the Lord will always rescue the righteous from trials of the unrighteous and protect them from the judgment and punishment of the wicked, so we should not become slaves to sin but be liberated by the freedom that Jesus gives.

A Drifter: is otherwise known as a Rolling Stone, a wanderer or a tramp.

In Church life Lot was classified as a Drifter, because he was not strong enough to muster the will to do right things hence he followed the course of least resistance, So, he was so unlike his uncle Abram, who later became Abraham, He was not just an uncle but a foster father, because Lots father died young, so it was his Grand-father Terah and his Uncle Abram who mentored him.

It is said: it must have been hard on Lot to have lost his father at such a very tender age. He got so caught up in the moment that he failed to see the consequence of his actions by not developing a better sense of purpose, with regards to the values of his grand-father and his uncle who raised him. After he drifted away from the family values, his life took an ugly turn after he blended himself into the sinful culture of the day, so much so that he did not want to give it up after awhile.

Lot was called righteous in the New Testament according to 2nd. Peter 02:   7&8 because history judged him by the way he rebuked his children, and those around him, he was upset with their behavior, It is God's mercy why he was not consumed with the others, because forgiveness is one of His attributes; God who allows His mercy to rewrite our lives, without which we all would be eternally doomed.

What is the direction of our life today? Are we heading in the right direction? Toward God, or away from Him, if you are a drifter, then the choice to follow God may seems difficult, but it is the only choice that put all other choices in a different light.

Are we allowing other people to determine our destiny like Lot's two daughters, who had drunken him then lie with him in order to protect the family name and justified their actions one with another for the satisfaction of their own lust. I am afraid of some justifications we make for the wrongs we have committed, and the efforts to cast the blame on others.

Lot could say I was drunk on both occasions and didn't know what was happening, while the two daughters might have said, you did not expose us early enough, and now there is no other available man in the family, to carry on the family name. So!!, Even though Lot was a successful businessman, yet when faced the choices of real life he did not stand up well; however God wants us to do more, and be more than a drifter, but to be firm in our faith and a good influence to others.

When we look how God has been good to Lot, even after all that he had done, he robbed his uncle Abram, and had the opportunity of enjoying the great blessings of Canaan yet he choose to drift to the wicked city of Sodom and even then God allowed angels to hold his hands that of his wife and two daughters and pulled them away from the burning city of Sodom; he was given the choice of getting up to the mountain of the little city nearby as recorded in: **Genesis 19:16**

Whenever we get into desperation we are likely to do things we would not normally have done. The two daughters thought that they would not get the chance to marry again and the family name needs to be preserved, but their uncle Abraham was not too far away and he was the person who was blessed. and received the promise to make the family name great, so that compromise could have been avoided; but they adopted the traits and lifestyle of the people of Sodom and allowed their culture and lifestyle it to get the better of them.

Look what has happened to Lot's two children who were born in incest, they became two nations who were, and still are enemies of Israel to this day. (**The Amorites** were an ancient Semitic-speaking people from Syria who also occupied large inhabitants of Canaan, before Assyria connected with the mountainous region **now called** Jebel Bishri which Some**time** later was referred to the Old Assyrian Empire.

The Moabites and the Ammonites, they are both located on the coast of the Jordon River, and Israel never conquered them because of the family connections, Moses wanted to conquer them, but he had plenteous mercy toward them. Moab is the name of an ancient kingdom that is *today* located in the modern state of Jordan. The *Moabite* capital was Dibon. According to the Hebrew *Bible*, Moab was often in conflict with its Israelite neighbors to the west.

Conclusion

We however need to be reminded that even though God is a faithful God, he will not hold His anger forever, because He is a Jealous God. He wants us to always make Him our focus and not to gaze on anyone else, of drift from his commandment; but to look fulsomely in his wonderful face, so that the things of this earth will always grow dim in light of His glory and grace.

Focus

To focus is to make something the center of their attraction, while, to focus on God is to make and have Him not only as the center of attraction but being our everything, and from preventing everything else from stealing our attention. We have to acknowledge that it is only God who can help us to get it right; for we can't even walk without Him holding our hands. So I will encourage each reader to let him lead us entirely, for those who follow where He leads are more than conquerors.

God Bless.

Chapter 48
There Is Nothing New Under The Sun

Read: Ecclesiastes 01:10 "Is there anything whereof it may be said, See, this is new? It has been already of old time, which was before us. **(In 977 B. C.)** The wise man Solomon wrote those wo: **Zechariah 09:09** "Rejoice greatly, O daughter of Zion, shout O daughter of Jerusalem, behold the King cometh unto thee; he is just, and having salvation; lowly, and riding upon an ass, and a colt the fold of an ass."

READ NT. St. Mark 11:07, 09, 11; "And they brought the colt to Jesus, and cast their garments on Him and he sat upon him, and they went before him and they that followed, cried, saying, Hosanna, blessed is he that cometh in the name of the Lord, and Jesus entered into Jerusalem, and into the temple, and when He had looked round about upon all things, and now the evening-tide was come, He went out unto Bethany with the twelve."

During the 2020 Easter Season, there was an unusual celebration due to the COVID-19 Pandemic, and persons were not able to congregate psychically as per usual. The importance of the season will still be upheld by most Christians. The triumphal entry of Jesus into Jerusalem on Palm Sunday serves as a reminder that people have a tendency to change their outlook on things, also their opinion of people overtime, however this time around as the world is going through this crisis let us remain focus on our Savior and avoid the distractions. That was **487 B.C.** later in **A.D 33** *(487+33=)* **520** years later it was fulfilled.

Nb. The very same persons, who shouted hosanna on Sunday in the triumphal entry of Jesus, they shout again on Friday of the same week, but the tone, the language, and the commitment was different.

People are the same everywhere: inconsistent, easily shaken, and such-like.

Today I will venture to address three basic points of restriction, that are biblically based, I am sure there are more occasions than these. The scripture shows that the world, whether in parts or in whole got **restriction** notices before, it is clear that on every occasion there were results.

1. **Read Matthew 10:5-7** Jesus gave His twelve disciples a restricted Mission. Jesus said: **V.5** "Go not in the way of the Gentiles," and into the City of the Samaritans enter ye not. But go rather to the lost sheep of the house of Israel, and as ye go, preach, saying: "The kingdom of heaven is at hand." History has proven that this is not the first time that persons have been restricted. The St. Matthew account states that special groups were given Restricted Mission based on Era, it was not yet time to minister to the Gentile population, or to go into the Cities of the Samaritan (The Gentiles were the None Jews) (the Samaritans were, a race that resulted from the intermarriages between the Jews and the Gentiles) they were known in some circles as *half-cast.* **Restriction:** limitation, constraint, control. (That restriction was a racial one.)

2. *(Gulf)* The gulf referred in **St. Luke 16: 22-26,** which is described as: a *profound depth in the sea; a deep hallow chasm. Brings to bear what happed in the discourse of* the rich man and Lazarus, in another clear occasion of standards of living, one that is maintained by wealth and poverty, as a social barrier; there has always been a notion that the rich feel, act or

perform at a level which is rated as if they are better than the rest. When the rich man looked at Lazarus in Abraham's bosom he cried to Father Abraham to send Lazarus to dip the tip of his finger in water and quench his tongue. That was so because the tables turned, **V.26** states, "that between you and us there is a great **gulf** fixed, so that they which would pass from hence to you cannot, neither can they pass to us; that would come from thence."

It is not so much the fast starters, nor the swift runners who usually win the race, especially a long race, but rather it is those who can endure to the end of the race usually wins. The rich man had his good times in the earlier part of his life, but at the end stage he ended up where he did want to be. It is not so much the runners but the winners. ***The Gulf then is what separates us. (Sin separates)***

3. **Leprosy:** Is a chronic infectious bacterial disease affecting skin and nerves, resulting in mutilations and deformities, moral corruption or contagion.

Up until 1940s Leprosy was still raging in some countries, for example India, Indonesia and other places. An account is given: According to **Leviticus 13: 08-17** once an individual was suspected to have the *leprosy* disease he or she was taken to the priest for examination at which point the priest ruled whether the patient be freed or insolated.

Leprosy has tormented humans throughout recorded history, For example, in Europe during the Middle-ages, **leprosy sufferers** had to wear special clothing. They were supposed to **ring a bell** to warn others that they were too close; so they were even supposed to walk on a particular side of the road, depending on the direction of the wind. It would seem to me that the disease could be air borne.

So there were occasions when there were isolations where the lepers had to remain by themselves until they were fully restored. A clean bill of health had to be given to them by the priest, before they could return to their villages, or be allowed in the Sanctuary. Those three occasions can be liken to the virus of today where we have to be apart as if there is really a great gulf between us and if a person is infected they have to be quarantined for a certain period of time and be tested twice by the medical team and get a negative result at least twice before any reunion with family and or community would be possible.

The lesson learnt is that there is nothing new under the sun. The point is the rules must be followed. The medical experts even though, still learning about this new virus; they have the expertise so we need to obey our leaders.

- Leprosy is synonymous to sin; sin can only be cleansed by the blood of Jesus.
- **The great Gulf between us**. Can be likened unto relationships and the responsibilities that come with choices. (but be assured that we will reap whatever we sow)
- **Era.** A divine appointment for a certain period of time. So Sisters and Brothers. the Jews had their opportunities, then it ceased, we are now in the Gentile's dispensation. This Dispensation will one day be closed, so all Non~Jews will have our Freedom expire, and the gate of mercy will be once again open for the unbelieving Jew. Our day of Salvation I now, **so**. let us do our best regarding our salvation. I have never dreamt of an experience like this. The good thing is: God is still our refuge and strength and our very present help in trouble. So let us rest securely in Him, for the Lord is our rock and in Him we can hide
- **Song** Hide me oh my Saviour hide until the storms of life is pass.

Chapter 49
Taking Domination Over The Family

Joshua is often referred to as one of the greatest Fathers, and National Leaders; of over one million persons who left Egypt, and were heading to Canaan the Promised Land. Joshua was one of the two only persons who reached it. The others did not survived the wilderness journey and experience, however, their offspring who were born in the wilderness entered, along with Caleb and Joshua, after he proved the goodness of the Lord; he pledged: "But as for me and my house, we will serve the Lord." **Joshua 24:15.**

Joshua took the responsibility as a father seriously, so he made it abundantly clear that he was in charge of his home, he made a declaration regarding the faith of his family, so he said: (We will not allow any foreign god to take our place, because it is You Lord that we love.)

The make-up of the Hebrew's family differed from ours today is some ways, as follows:

The English Dictionary: describes it as: "A fundamental Social groups in society consisting of a Man, a Woman and their offspring, or people of the same lineage. (Regardless of their marital status)

The Bible Dictionary: The Hebrew's family was much larger than our families today, in that, it included the father, his parents, his wife and children, daughters-in-law, sons-in-law, slaves, and guests. The parent's authority was so respected, that if any one dishonored them, they were punishable by death according to **Exodus 21:15 – 17.**

The Purpose: The purpose of the family as God instructs, "Is to procreate and replenish the earth. The family unit denotes the First Church; it is there that God expects to get the most of His praise and Glory from, and in a consistent way. It is to this end hat Joshua in his final message to Israel (Chapter 24:15 said): As for me and my house we will serve the Lord. This is synonymous to the thought: The family that prays together stays together.

I will attempt to highlight four Primary Functions of the Family, they are:

1. Communication

Communication can be done in different ways, depending on where you are, to whom you speak, and how clearly understood you are and how much you are accepted and appreciated. Whichever way it is done, it is necessary in order to foster harmony in the unit, where parents owe children this appreciation, and children owe it to their parents; it is also essential for clear understanding. Trust, safety, and clear instructions and openness are important because: Communication is to love, as blood is to life.

2. Appreciation

Whoever is in charge of planning the family activities, should include, systems or appreciation for each member of the family, this does not have to be an expensive gesture as we sometimes think, it is essential to note that everyone needs appreciation.

3. Commitment

It is important to note, that we should make commitments for family time, and they should be honored, a similar sense of purpose among families is also necessary, this usually results in a better family life and family success. (eg. going to the beach, having picnics, taking vacations away from home, and above all, pray together).

4. Marriage

Ephesians 05:21-28 Speaks to that aspect of the family's life, and described it as one of the high points of the family's achievements, it is recommended that it be approached with much prayer and care, because of the contractual arrangements and the level of commitments required in this arrangement. Marriage was ordained by God, blessed and sanctioned by him, and Christ compared it to his love for the church, which He gave himself for it, that he might sanctify it by the washing of water by the word.

Ephesians 06:01-09. Gives a complete coverage of the entire domestic life; which includes not just the blood relatives, but also the hired servants, if that was the case. It further specify by single point accountability, the roles and responsibilities of each member of the family, in a manner that fosters peace, harmony in order for the wellbeing and success of all.

Conclusion

There is nothing so pronounced as a father's declaration over his family (as priest) by demanding sober living, delighting in the success of each member of the family, suggest changes and transformation for the family's success, celebrate success and outstanding achievements, and be there for them when there are failures, always communicate clearly his anticipation, and demonstrate his feelings genuinely.

If as parents, we start to focus more on our families, and teach and practice the better values to our children, then: the

teachers, the pastors, the counselors, our parents our spouses, our neighbors, our employers, the law-enforcers, and the governments would certainly have far less troubles, and we would all enjoy life at the higher end of the sociological and economical ladder. All parents need to take the full responsibility to instill the right values in our children, at the earliest possible point of our children's lives, always depending on God as our guide, because the scripture says: "except the lord builds the house, we labour in vain that build it, we rise up early and set up late, then eat the bread of sorrow." One of the greatest and most guaranteed ways to have and maintain victories and successes in our families is to reverence and fear God, and let Him direct our steps.

Chapter 50
Singleness With Contentment

The Disciples Study Bible highlights **22** Spiritual Gifts however; **Singleness and Creative Communication** are not included in that discourse, but the COGOP Teacher's Guide of 2018 highlights those two giftedness which would expand that number to **24** gifts it is to be noted that this list is in no was exhausted.

	Spiritual Gifts	Spiritual Disciplines
1.	Prophesying	Prayer
2.	Serving	Fasting
3.	Teaching	Meditation
4.	Encouraging	Submission
5.	Contribution	Service
6.	leadership	Study
7.	Showing Mercy	Confession
8.	Wisdom	Journaling
9.	Knowledge	Solution
10.	Faith	Simplicity
11.	Healing	Worship
12.	Miraculous Powers	Guidance
13.	Prophecy	Celebration
14.	Distinguishing Spirits	Transformation
15.	Tongues	
16.	Interpretation	
17.	Teaching	
18.	Administration	
19.	Apostleship	
20.	Prophecy	
21.	Evangelism	
22.	Pastoral Teaching	

23.	Singleness	
24.	Creative Communication	

The matter of singleness as recorded in **1st. Corinthians 07:32-40 Is** very clear that it has always been a great concern that Paul had, even though the Holy Scriptures gave some clear conditionality pertaining to singleness, then he gave four main categories. (For both Males and Females)

1. He who is unmarried cares for the things of the Lord. How he may please Him.
2. But he who is married, cares for the things of the world, how he may please his wife.

But note, there is a difference between a wife and a virgin.

1. The unmarried woman cares about the things of the Lord, that she may be holy both in body and spirit.
2. But she who is married, care for the things of the world, how she may please her husband.

V. 35. States: "And this I say for your own profit, not that I may put a leash on you, for what may be proper, and for you to serve the Lord without distraction, and especially if you would pass the flowers of your youth, let him do what he wishes, it is not a sin, it is better to marry." (The Hugs Bible)

Never-the-less he who stands steadfast in his heart, having no necessity, and has no power over his own will, and determine in his heart that he may keep his virgin, does well, so he who gives her hand in marriage does better, having no necessity.

The word singleness is not confined to one who has never marry, but may also be applied to the widows, widowers, or divorced, the separated and in some instances a Common law relationship, therefore the fact that one falls in any of the categories afore mentioned, should be viewed in light of the 1^St^. **Corinthians 07: 32-40** discourse; which further defines the condition of a virgin to be both: (male and female) and refers to anyone who has never been engaged in a sexual intercourse. This status of singleness; otherwise, being **unmarried** appears only **four times** in the English Bible, and all four times are to be found in the New Testament, as compared to the word married and appears **twenty eight times**, if the feature of weights is being applied then, this may be saying that the populace would be of greater concern about being married than being single.

I know from my research that some singles is better than marriage, in the case where : one or both partners are independent, the matter of independence, comes into play when one or both parties lived on their own for an extended period of time, especially if they are professionals, and can managed on their own financially, in that case, each person usually feels that they are in charge, and so they usually want to do things independently, as they were accustomed to, so to be told by someone else you can't, or you shouldn't do that, or you shouldn't do it that way, usually becomes problematic, therefore much prayer and counseling are always needed in the approach to marriage, but more-so in cases with this kind of uniqueness regarding prolonged periods of singleness.

Respect

Being both respectable, respectful and appreciative, are some of the characteristics that determines the harmony, continuity and success of a marriage relationship, because they give rise to how husbands and wives see each other, listen to, and speak to each other, most of all, a certain amount of dependence is highly necessary in a marriage relationship, in order for partnership, to come into full play.

Compatibility

Compatibility is paramount to harmony; because if it is absent then there will be no commonality or sameness and if so, the partners can become distant from each other, also a relationship like that has the potential to become adversarial to each other, and in that case, the objectivity of the marriage would not be met.

Conclusion

Contentment is one of the hallmarks of marriage, therefore when the fourteen Spiritual Disciplines mentioned earlier, are practiced by both parties, then it is much easier to live together in harmony, all of the disciplines except journaling (which is record keeping) should be realized, because, love keeps no records of wrongs, so our errors should be dealt with urgently and respectfully, because when proper communication is done, it builds a good platform for couples to stand on, and it should be done from the start.

God Bless.

Chapter 51
Marriage, One Of The High Points Of Family Achievements

The Apostle Paul spoke of Marriage, in 1st. Corinthians 07: 01 to 40 where he addressed the whole family. The advice he gave to the married was excellent, even though he said that: "he spoke not by command, but by permission of the things that they should do, (this might have been because he was not married) and in verse 07 he made reference to the point, that if one choose to remain unmarried, for the gospel's sake or even to be like him; Paul. Then that is classified as one segment of the giftedness.

Marriage is viewed internationally as a high point of the family's achievements, this is so in most sectors of society, among nations, races and most Religious groups, where marriage is accepted, parents looked forward to their adult children getting married, upon reaching adulthood and are otherwise prepared, rather than diverting to common-law relationships and or alternative lifestyles; because some children have yielded to themselves teachers having itching ears and have twisted Biblical Truths into fables and have taught and are teaching them to others. They have even put sweeteners in the fables, in order to entice others by calling marriage an outdated tradition. So we should stand on the original, all times undisputed words of God according to: **St. Mark 10: 09 and Hebrews 13: 04**

I will refer to one of the Quotes from the Matthew Henry's Collection as follows: "Be not afraid of saying too much in the praise of God, all the dangers lies in saying too little" So let us continue to teach the right values to our children. The reference made previously: "What God has joined together let no man put asunder is saying to us: "God has joined together one man to one woman for life" Marriage is usually celebrated with family members and friends, which was and is usually done with much rejoicing; however there can be several reasons for rejoicing I will mention a few.

1. In the case of a daughter, her maintenance expenses are transferred to the son-In-law.
2. The family's legacy will remain in the family, rather than being passed on to strangers.
3. If a double-barrel name title is allowed then the family name will live on.
4. When the grandchildren are born in wedlock. It speaks well for the family's reputation. (although alternative lifestyles say otherwise)
5. Preserving the Moral Standards that are taught.
6. Fulfilling the word of the Holy Scriptures, as is stated in **Proverbs 17: 06**: The glory of the aged is their grandchildren.
7. There will be reinforcement to speak with the enemies within their gates **Psalm 127: 03-05**

It is important to teach the Biblical values to our children, and teach them by example rather than by instructions, because children live what they learn, in the world around us are many different directions, but we should teach them the right ones.

1. Moral directions
2. Religious directions
3. Safety directions
4. And the directions to success.

They can, and they may depart from them fully or in part, but the wise man Solomon said in **Proverb 22: 06:** "Train up the child in the way they should go: and when he is old he will not depart from it."

It is a known fact that we live in a changing world, also that parental influences are weakening due to, Rights, all of a sudden everybody has rights, regardless of opinions and ideas, we are however duty-bound to teach the God Given rules, especially to our children; it is better to teach them and they are rejected, than not teach them and we are found wanting. **1st. Kings 09:04** States: "And if thou will walk before me, as David thy father walked in the integrity of his heart, and in uprightness to do according to all that I have commanded you, and will keep my statures and my judgments. Then he would inherit the kingdom of Israel as was promised to your father David." If the average clause is applied then some of our children will stand up well, others may choose to do otherwise, due to different things, example the difference between nature and nurture as to which is stronger. So if our children are going to bow to pressure and influences from their peers, and do the wrong thing, then there is going to be a en extensive departure from the laws of God; but there will always remain even a lingering trait of the original teaching

For more detail on the traditions of Biblically Sound Marriages see my Book: **A Unique Passion for Healthy Marriages, Part 03, Pages 15-17.**

Conclusion

Often we talk about what the good reasons for getting married are, but sometimes we don't say much about what the reasons for getting married should not be; one should not get married for the following reasons:

1. Simple for just a status change.
2. Or for a name change.
3. For getting even with friends.
4. To legalize sexual intercourse.
5. To have children.

6. Or for reward for a good deed.
7. For opportunity to migrate (Business Marriage)
8. For an opportunity to leave the family home.
9. For someone to take on you responsibility.
10. Nor for religious reasons.

Marriage should only be done, because two persons are genuinely in love with each other, because marriages built on any other premise will definitely not last, I don't even support the practice, that because two Christians fall from grace and get themselves messed up, they should get married for a cover-up, or for two persons to get married because there are children in the relationship. I maintain the point that marriages are to be deliberate, it must be planned for, and both parties are to be prepared for it, so much so, that each person should be able to take something to the marriage, not necessarily wealth, or material things, but at least a skill to make him or her employable.

We have a tendency to put the Cart before the horse, but whenever one does that, then there is definitely going to be bundling, the ideal thing is: the horse must always be in front of the cart. I recommend the Garden of Eden's model for families; when God planted the Garden in Eden, "He engaged the services of Adam to both dress it and keep it" It is clear that preparation should precede the process of procreation, and we should make sure that the garden is fully grown, and fruited, before he or she takes on the responsibility to start a meaningful relationship See: **Genesis 02:15-18**. Therefore to whatever extent the multiplication gets, it will be manageable because provisions are already in place, therefore the family will not suffer lack. It is to this end, that I share the point that all aspirants should be able to impact their relationship in a rounded way, before getting married or starting a family. So, we need to qualify ourselves before we agree to start relationships; this preparation for marriage need to be effected in the following ways: mentally, physically, emotionally, spiritually and financially. It is in no way meant to be that only the wealthy should get married, but that basic financial qualification should precede marriage, in order to find the harmony it was intended to give.

Chapter 52
The Strong And Courageous Will Always Be Victorious

Reading lessons Numbers 14: 20-36 & Joshua 06: 01–25

It is important to note that (Those whom entered Canaan the Promised Land) were only persons under the age of twenty, the only two other persons who were older were: Caleb and Joshua (and they were the exception) All *persons below 20 years. Should be singing Joshua's song* (We are a chosen Generation)

It is important to note here that friendship can, and will influence our failures and / or successes, It is said that Caleb and Joshua were friends, and they were bound together by Minority Conviction; they were both convinced that they could fight and win any battle, contrary to the other ten Spies; they told Moses that: "Giants were in the land and to them and we are only like grass hoppers when compared to them". **Read Numbers13:30-33.** When we hang around persons with negative thoughts and attitudes, we can be engulfed by their behaviors, and unless we are very strong, they can help to make our life battles twice as hard, and our victories can become so difficult, or even impossible.

Numbers 13:1-16

The Lord told Moses to send men to explore the land of Canaan, and that there should be a leaders for every tribe; and they should enter the Land of Canaan as Spies.

#s	Tribe	Name	
1.	Ruben	Shammua **son** of Zaccur	
2.	Simeon	Shaphat **son** of Hori	
3.	Judah	Caleb **son** of Jephunneh	
4.	Issachar	Igal **son** of Joseph	
5.	Ephraim	Hosea son of **Nun (Joshua)**	
6.	Benjamin	**Palti son of Raphu**	
7.	Zebulun	Gaddiel **son** of Sodi	
8.	Manasseh	(A tribe of Joseph) Gaddie **son** of Sodi	
9.	Dan	Ammiel **son** of Gemalli	
10.	Asher	Sethur **Son** of Michael	
11.	Naphtali	Nabi **son** of Vopshi	
12.	Gad	Geuel **son** of Maki	

Numbers 14 24 states that "Because my servant Caleb had a different spirit and follow me wholeheartedly.

Joshua 06: 07 State I will bring him into the land he went to, and his descendant will inherit it" and God gave them a route toward the Red Sea.

Korah (Occupations were: A Levite & Tabernacle Assistant)

Numbers 16: 01-04 States that Korah was a popular leader but greed caused him to want to grab unto more than what was allotted to him, he suffered a bad fate.

READ Numbers 16:23-36 The ill-fate of those who rebelled against Moses Sp. V 31-35

He and his friends making a total of 250 Israelite men, well known Council Men conspired against Moses, the group came to Moses and Aaron and confronted them. (They thought that self acclaimed possession would rank them equal to Moses and Aaron. You can Read 16:03-39) the highlights of his statements boils down to 3 main points

1. You are no better than anyone else.
2. Everyone in Israel has been chosen of the Lord.
3. We don't need to obey you.

It is amazing to see how Korah twisted the two first two statements. (both are true to reach the wrong conclusion. one of the good things about Korah is, he was among the first to be chosen from among the Levites to special service in the tabernacle, but he fail to recognize the specific position that God placed him in, and the fight was against someone greater than Moses, and he allowed greed to blind his common senses.

The main lessons learnt from this experience is that (we should abide in their calling.

1. Don't let desire for what someone else has; make you discontented with what you already have.
2. Don't try to raise your own self esteem by attacking someone else's.
3. Don't use part of God's word to support what you want, rather than allowing its entirety to shape your wants.
4. Don't expect to find satisfaction in power and position, because God my just want to work through you in the position you are now in.

Moses told Korah, listen! The God of Israel has chosen and separated you as Levites, to stand between the people and me. Isn't that enough you want the priesthood. (Remember he that humbles himself shall be exalted, but he that exalted himself shall be a base)

Let us be positive in all our approach to life and especially our leaders.

Our courageousness, will give us the victories we desire.

Conclusion

Let us seek the peace of God, in our daily walk, it is sufficient to life and victories.

Romans 12:18 "If it is possible, as far as it depends on you, live at peace with every man." **(NIV)**

P - Practical in the midst of the storm.

E - Enough regardless.

A - Accessible to all.

C - Ceases not

E - Everlasting.

Chapter 53
Finding Solutions During A Crisis

Reading Acts 27:

A crisis: is a time of great danger to health, and life, with the potential to escalate. At this point: March 29, 2020 the peril at hand is, it is that the whole world will soon be affected and to make thing worst there is no treatment or VACCINE to combat the virus.

History has proven that from time to time the world has experienced and is experiencing an unusual spread of Viruses. There are billions of Viruses, some falling to earth and they fall daily. **To Date: March 29, 2020. The twelve (12) deadliest viruses on earth are: The Marbug Virus, Ebola, Rabies. HIV, Small Pox, Hantivarus, Influenza, Dengue, Rota Virus, SARS-COV, SARS- Cov-2, and MERS- COV. Otherwise called Corona Virus or COVID- 19.**

According to the WHO. Concerning the two most extreme conditions regarding disease: they are Epidemic and Pandemic

Epidemic: An epidemic is defined as follows: the brake out and spreading of diseases beyond normal conditions, it may be affecting several countries.

Pandemic: When a new disease breaks out and is spreading across the world without immunity, Vaccine or any ideal treatment. We are all on a ledge between anxiety and fear, but God is our refuge and strength ans a very present help in trouble.

	Names	Comments
1.	**Marburg Virus**	This was mostly in Germany, it affected workers who were exposed to infected monkeys in **1976, 1998, 2000 & 2005**
2.	**Ebola**	It was first discovered in the Democratic Republic of the Congo in **1976,** and in Sudan, West Africa and again in **2014**
3.	**Rabies**	It was first discovered in India and West Africa in **1920 i**t mostly affects the brain, but a Vaccine was created, if the patient is not treated they will die.
4.	**HIV**	HIV is the biggest killer to date it was first recognized in **1980,** however through the use of antiviral drugs the affected can live for yeas Nb. In every 25 adult in Africa is said to be HIV positive and much more than that have the Virus.
5.	**Small Pox**	Small Pox was around for ages in South Africa (thousands of years) it killed I out every 3 persons, those that live either had permanent scars or went blind, but in 1980 The WHO declared the whole world free from Small Pox.
6.	**Hantavirus**	**In 1950, 1993 & 2010** the four corners of USA was affected by a Deer mouse who was living in a home and infected more than 600 persons in the country, 36% of the persons affected died eventually that transmission is only done through droppings of infected animals

7.	**Influenza**	Influenza otherwise called Spanish Flue created havoc during the Flu season and have killed up to 500,000 per season, so, between **1918 and 2018** it has killed up-to 50 million people
8.	**Dengue**	Since **1950** Dengue was discovered in the Philippines and Thailand and later spread world- wide, it has affected between 50 and 100 millions. If the virus is left untreated, it can manifest symptoms like the Ebola virus. However in **2019** the USA developed a Vaccine for the virus.
9.	**ROTA Virus**	The Rota Virus has affected over 453,000 children under the age of five years and they died but in **2008,** but a vaccine is now available for it
10.	**SARS –Cov**	This virus first appeared in southern China in **2002** it then spread to 26 other countries, It is discovered to have emerged from bats. It has affected over 8,000 persons killed over **770** with a mortality rate of **91%**
11.	**SARS-Cov2**	**Since December 2019** the SARS-COV-2 now known as the Corona Virus from the Chinese city of Wuhan most likely came from the family of bats, through an intermediary animal then to human and later named **COVID 19** to date it has affected hundreds of thousands of people and has killed thousands and has affected almost the entire world

		The symptoms include dry cough, shortness of breath, fever, and eventually pneumonia.
12.	**MERS-Cov**	**From about 2012** the MERS-COV virus emerged in the Middle east and is known as the Middle East Respiratory Syndrome or MERS. It sparks an outbreak in Saudi Arabia and in South Korea in **2015** it belongs to the SARS-Cov. and SARS-COV family and likely originated from bats as well. It infects Camels then was passed on to humans. The symptoms are: fever, coughing and short of breath in the affected persons it has mortality rate of 30 % 40% this Virus the most lethal of the known Corona Viruses. The bad thing is: there is no approved treatment or vaccine to date.

This COVID 19 crisis that affects and threatened to affect the entire world shows the importance of community, in that it shows the benefits of unselfishness and or being our brother's keepers, the whole matter of Social distancing, an advanced Hygiene practice, being more family oriented, caring for the less fortunate's and the acknowledging of the frailties of man, I am not forced to think, that if humans can die so easily then why we have to create so much bombs and high powered weapons to kill us. If just a cough, a sneeze, some perspiration or touching or mingling can do it.

Our actions and our behaviors in the church must be paramount for the safety and success of the church. So the word fellowship and friendship come into scrutiny, in that, our every action just don't affect us as individual alone, but more so the local, national, and the general church. If we would closely evaluate our actions then some of the things we say, and or the things we do, we would not have done them, as Adam alone sinned and the whole world suffer for it. So it took one man alone to give the whole world hope. As we closely look at the process of contagion with this deadly virus, we should that behavior is learnt, so whatever we do will influence the behavior of others. So, let us use this medium to say, a church is as good as its members, and my actions will influence the outcome one way or the next. What is my intension? Do I want to impact the church and or the kingdom in a positive way? So then should I continue on the path I am on, or do I change course?

When you see these things, look up for our redemption draws near.

Chapter 54
Food For Survival

From the beginning of time, food was known as the staff of life, in the Genesis account as is recorded in **chapter 01: 29-31** it is very noticeable that before God created man he made food for man's sustenance; that includes the seeds, the herbs, the fishes and other types of flesh for food for mankind, He did not only provide for mankind, but he provided for everything that liveth, therefore there was no excuse regarding survival. Then in **1760 B.C.** Jacob upon reaching Bethel (previously called luz) he receiving his blessings, as a part of the blessing, he had a dream, as recorded in **Genesis 28:19-22** when he woke up, he vowed to the lord saying: "If God will be with me, and will keep me in this way that I go, and will give me bread to eat and raiment to put on, so that I come again unto My father's house in peace, then shall the Lord be my God, And this stone, which I have set for a pillar, shall be God's house, and of all that Thou shalt give me I will surely give the tent unto Thee."

It is evident here again, that in the asking for the things that matters most; food was, and still is, among man's ten greatest needs; in the vow that Jacob made, a portion was pledged to God for the sustenance of the priestly tribe; sharing is a vital part of the Christian's obligation and should not only be toward the priestly tribe, but should also be toward the less-fortunate.

The **Exodus 16: 01- 36** account which was made about **1805 B.C.** when Israel journeyed from Elim toward Sinai, on reaching the Desert of Sin, which is the midpoint between the two stations, the people murmured against Moses and Aaron saying: we could have died in

Egypt at the hand of the Lord, but at least, we sat around pots of meat in Egypt, eating all we wanted, yet you have brought us out into the desert to starve this entire assembly to death. (NIV) God fed them with Quails and mamma for forty years, until they reached the borders of Canaan. **Exodus16:35**.

People are the same now like they were then, they complained for water in the Desert of Shur, because the water was bitter. (Marah) later they complained for food (a different generation alltogether) forty-five years later, we saw the same human needs) Jacob made his vow at Bethel (which included food) Jacob made his vow in **1760 B.C.** and in about **A.D. 34** approximately **1,794** years later, the disciples asked Jesus to teach them how to pray. Jesus responded to them in **St. Matthew 06: 09-13**. Which is today known as: "The Lord's Prayer" **V.11** states: "Give us this day our daily bread"

Quite a few prayers were included in the Lord's Model Prayer Example:

Read St. Matthew 06:13.

Verse 09: Worship the Lord in Prayer

Verse 09: Seeking to do God will

Verse 09: Prayer of submission

Verse 11: Prayer for food

Verse 12: Prayer for our forgiveness

Verse 12: Prayer to be able to forgive others

Verse 13: Prayer to overcome temptation

Verse 13: Prayer to be delivered from evil

Verse 13: Prayer to know God's Power and

Verse 13: Prayer for us to be willing to glorify God always.

The various types of prayer cannot be exhausted, but there are those that God expects us to do daily, and that was why he gave His disciples the procedure and the frequency. We need to eat food and drink water daily, in order to remain healthy, because eating and drinking are as important as rest and sleep, the medical experts say: we may live for days without food and water, according to: **REUTERS / Francois Lenoir**: "Humans need food and water to survive, at least 60% of the adult body is made of water. A human can go without food for **about three weeks** but would typically only last **three to four days** without water. Mar 8, 2018"

(We are unlike the Reptiles) example, an alligator eats only once per week, usually it goes for a big catch and that is enough to keep it for that one week period, because it is a cold blooded creature, we have to eat more often because our digestive systems and organs are different; similar to our natural eating habits, where we eat several times per day, Jesus desires us to pray to Him frequently every day, Job said in **Chapter 23:12.** "Neither have I gone back from the commandments of Thy lips; I have esteemed the words of His mouth more than my necessary food."

Save and except for Spiritual occasions such as fasting and prayer, we should eat on a regular basis. If we are on fasting, then, that is an exception; as fasting is one of the Spiritual Disciplines, fasting transports us unto the presence of the Lord where we communicate with Him through prayer, some person's needs and commitments are different; they can go for long periods of fasting, due to their situations, expectations and / or commitments.

Conclusion

Every Christian should develop a certain discipline for our prayer life, reading and devotional life (Spiritual food) even in a more meaningful way, than that of our natural lifestyle is set-up; even if we don't have, or can't find food to eat, because we lack, we will always find spiritual food, once we look in the right direction; Jesus told the disciples some deep truth, at a point when they had a great misunderstanding. **St. John 6:31-37** "For the bread of God, is he which cometh down from heaven, and gives life unto the world. And Jesus said unto them, I am the bread of life, he that cometh unto me, shall never hunger; and he that that believeth on me shall never thirst; and again Jesus makes it available to all. He even said in **Malachi 03:10**: "Prove Me now, saith the Lord of hosts. If I will not open the windows of Heaven, and pour you out a blessing, that there shall not be room enough to receive it."

The natural Food is necessary to preserve life and prevent physical death. And Spiritual food is necessary to prevent spiritual death and preserve the spirit life. So Job said I esteem it more than my necessary food.

Chapter 55
God! In Tough Times

It is occasions like these that cause us to find innovative ways to share a discourse. **VIA Social Media** I said to you previously, let's assemble together as often as we can, because the times may come when we might not be able to do so, but never thought that it would be so soon, nor in such a critical manner, this is also in keeping with the Advice to members: "that we should attend every regular service as far as possible"

Read: *2nd. Timothy 03:01*: "This know also, that in the last days, **perilous** times shall come"

Tough Times: Perilous, hard, dangerous, hard-hitting, or rough times.

And certainly without a shadow of a doubt, this is a real hard time. Almost everyone is either fearful, anxious or both.

It is situations like these that the quality of our make-up is tested, by this I mean our patience, our endurance and our stability, our fears, and the will to stay within the boundaries of the Christian faith. Paul said in **2nd. Timothy 02:03** "Thou therefore endure hardness as a good soldier of Jesus Christ." Hardness comes in various ways (To each his own).

Fear is one of the most serious life's Threatening Situations that faces everyone, and Christians are not exempt. So, be it known that fear is not of God, for the scripture says according to **2nd. Timothy 01:07**: "For God has not given us the spirit of fear; but of power, and of love and of a sound mind" In terrible and troublesome times like these, fears will even cause sleeplessness, it can take our appetite, steal our hopes and cripples our security. It is only in God we will find the solace and comfort that can remedy these situations, hence it is high time to draw closer to Him and remain there for the rest of our lives.

It is indeed shameful to see some of the thing that we sometimes trade our Salvation for. I am fully aware that some of the statements made are easier said than done.   For it is only when we are so hard pressed that we realize how difficult a situation we are entangled in. this then tells me, that we have to walk by faith and not by sight, and to always depend on God as our guide.

My Sisters and brothers, I implore you to total commitment to God because I was shocked myself of how I came out so clean, out of a recent confrontation, this is unlike the way people behave when really, really put to the test, But God, in every temptation he make a way for us to escape. I am reassured that the words of God are powerful to the pulling down of the strong hold s of the enemy. So we only need to rely on Him. I can safely say He shelters us like the hens shelter their chicken.

When we face our tough times, be reminded of David's experiences, in particular **Psalm 23:01-06** "Yea though I walk through the valley of the shadow of death; I will fear no evil; for Thou are with me, and Thy rod and Thy staff, they comfort me, and prepares a table before me in the presence of mine enemies, and anoint our heads with oil; and make our cups run over, not just for today or this time but it ends with some conditions. Which exacts some personal commitments: And I shall dwell in the house of the Lord forever. Clearly if we keep our end of the bargain even in the toughest of time, God will keep His.

It is the Same God a morning, Same God a evening, Massa God a God.

As we go through this global crisis with **COVID-19** God remains our only Refuge and strength and our present help in times of trouble. A few years I tried to hide from CHICKEN GUNIA but it found me, although we are people of faith let us use wisdom and follow the guidelines of the medical experts, and trust God for He is the real Protector and in Him only we can hide.

Right now we are living on a ledge between (being alone; maybe with just our immediate family) or run the risk of contagion by hanging out with the crowd, the choice is always going to be our, but good sense say: get wisdom which is the principal thing, but in all you're getting, get understanding. The Corona Virus is no respecter of persons, it respects neither Young nor old, rich nor poor, black nor white, and for sure, Status is no match for her. we were told earlier that it will only affect the seniors and or persons with underlining illnesses, that has now being proven to be wrong, we also learnt that United States Congress men and women are affected, also Prime Ministers and their spouses from the various jurisdictions, as a matter of fact Kingdom activities had to be scaled down in this week due to the regulations concerning crowd gathering.

We have got to find innovative ways to do things because barbers, hair dressers and other groups of persons who usually offer their services to us, they are now restricted, and may only work by appointment, so, most of us will either have to do without them or do them ourselves.

There is also no barrier where nations and countries are concern it is interesting to note that out of the 197 countries in the world we were the 120th. Country to be affected with the other 77 countries incidents free, but by Thursday March 20, 2020 a matter of ten days 32 others were affected, leaving only 45 not yet pronounced. It is predicted that all countries will be affected (So then, none shall escaped)

Conclusion

Psalm 46: 01-11 "God is our refuge and strength,

> *A very present help in trouble*
> *Therefore let us not fear, because there is a river,*
> *The streams that shall make glad the city of God.*
> *The Lord of host is with us, and the God of Jacob is our*
> *refuge.*
> *Be still and know that I am God. He said*
> *This time of trouble is to exalt Him in the earth*

Be assured my sisters and brothers, that the Lord of host is with us and that, the God of Jacob is our refuge.

As we join forces together in Prayer for God to heal our Nation Jamaica Land we Love If we humble ourselves and pray and seek His face and turn from our wicked ways then He will hear from Heaven and will heal our land.

So let us pray.

We need to ask ourselves these questions.

What example am I? Am I the kind of person whose actions are based on the following?

1. Kindness.
2. Faithfulness
3. Generosity
4. Sympathy
5. Understanding
6. And love?

If our lives fit in with the above traits, then we are not only blessed, but highly favoured, those things can only make us powerful, virtuous and highly productive women of God, and can be a force to reckon with, the church needs women of positive influence, kingdom builders, examples to the believers in love, in spirit, in purity and in virtue. When we rise to those levels we only need to depend on God to continue to order our steps, because we can't even walk without him holding our hands.

God Bless.

Other Books by Author

A Unique Passion for Healthy Marriages

What is marriage? What does marriage entail and is it meant to be long term? This book details the answers to these questions and more. Written in the form of an interview these questions are addressed outlining what is expected in a marriage. We need to think of how life will be with a partner, how to overcome challenges we will face and how to resolve conflicts and misunderstandings. This book promotes Communication as the key ingredient to successful relationships and answers the question of whether or not marriage is still relevant.

Autobiography and Pictorials of a Fulfilled Life

William was born in the district of Marlie Hill Manchester. He spent his formative years there. He received his early education at the Marlie Hill Elementary School. He later migrated to May Pen, Clarendon in 1977 and currently resides at Mineral Heights. He boasted being married to Arlene since September 02, 1978, the union produced two children.

William is a Christian and is actively involved in serving in the following capacities: Administrative Bishop for Clarendon South COGOP, consisting of twenty-three Churches and pastor for the following churches: Hayes & Bustamante Highway. He has served in the following churches: Palmers Cross, Rocky Point, Longsville, Free Town, and Old Monymusk. He served as interim pastor for Savannah Cross and Mt. Airy and He is also serving on four National boards (between 2005 and now).

He is a Marriage Officer since March 1998, author, volunteer in the Clarendon Chapter of the Jamaica Red Cross Society.

He holds a Master of Arts in Religion and Diploma in Christian Leadership from the Gordon Conwell Theological Seminary (USA), Diploma in Practical Theology from the International Theological Seminary (USA), Diploma in Practical English from the International Correspondence School (USA), Diploma in Religious Education from the Bible Training Institute COGOP (Kingston, Jamaica), Diploma in Production and Operations Management from the IMP (Now University of the Caribbean), Diploma in Automotive and Diesel Mechanics from the National Technical School NTS. California, USA.

In addition he holds numerous Certificates and Licenses from other leading and recognized organizations in Jamaica and abroad; which includes: the Insurance College of Insurance and Professionals (Kingston Jamaica), the American College of Insurance and Professionals (USA), Jamaica Institute of Management (JIM) (Kingston Jamaica), The Job Bank (Kingston Jamaica), the Marriage Unit (Ministry of Justice), Church of God of Prophecy (Cleveland Tennessee USA).

About the Book

No man is an island, no man stands alone. We are all made up of each other and need to be supplied by our neighbours, so we learn from each other that those of us in leadership or aspiring for leadership must first recognize:

1. That we are called by God.
2. That the call must be acknowledged by the individual.
3. The call must be sanctioned by our superior.

Then the three stages of the call would be fulfilled, and that would be the best foundation for one to build on. The rest of the work continues as follows: Paul said in 2 Timothy 2:15: "Study to show thyself approved unto God, a workman that needeth not be ashamed rightly dividing the word of truth."

A good leader must be well read, and have a broad view on the varying types of leadership that exist, and know his/her own personality, and how to relate to others. He/she should have a good interpretation of the Scriptures, but above everything, he or she should have a Spiritual connection with God, through the power of the Holy Spirit. The author hopes that through the sharing of his spiritual journey, others will find help through reading, and will be better able to inspire others.

William D. Hutchinson is a husband for over forty-two years, a father of two children and three grandchildren, a pastor, marriage officer, counselor, church administrator, national worker of COGOP, and the author of two other books: "A Unique Passion for Healthy Marriages" and "Autobiography and Pictorials of a Fulfilled Life." He has over thirty-six years in pastoral Ministry and enjoys a good relationship with his colleagues and pastorates.